BERLITZ®

ISTANBUL
and the Aegean Coast

1990/1991 Edition

D1052341

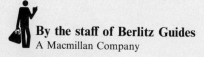

By the staff of Berlitz Guides
A Macmillan Company

Berlitz Trademark Reg. U.S. Patent Office and other countries.
Library of Congress Catalog Card No. 86-80081.

Printed in Switzerland by Weber S.A., Bienne.

5th Printing
1990/1991 Edition

How to use our guide

- All the **practical information**, hints and tips that you will need before and during the trip start on p. 102.

- For **general background**, see the sections The City and the People, p. 6, and A Brief History, p. 12.

- All the principal sights to visit are described between pp. 28 and 86. Our own choice of sights most highly recommended is pinpointed by the Berlitz traveller symbol.

- A rundown of suggestions of **purchases** to look out for is on pp. 86–90.

- **Entertainment** is described between pp. 90 and 93.

- **Sports** figure on pp. 93–96.

- The pleasures and possibilities of **eating out** in Istanbul and on the Aegean coast are covered between pp. 96 and 101.

- An index on pp. 127–128 lists the place names occurring in the guide.

Although we make every effort to ensure the accuracy of all the information in this book, changes occur incessantly. We cannot therefore take responsibility for facts, prices, addresses and circumstances in general that are constantly subject to alteration. Our guides are updated on a regular basis as we reprint, and we are always grateful to readers who let us know of any errors, changes or serious omissions they come across.

Text: Catherine McLeod
Staff Editor: Barbara Ender
Photography: Daniel Vittet
Layout: Doris Haldemann
We wish to express our thanks to the Turkish Ministry of Tourism and Culture, especially to Mr. Cengiz Taner, for their kind cooperation. We are also grateful to Nezihe Aygen and Nurdan Üstman, Elif Taşkıran, Stella Vayne and Richard Grummitt, for their help in the preparation of this guide.
Cartography: **Falk** Falk-Verlag, Hamburg.

Contents

Cover picture: Blue Mosque.
Photo pp. 2–3: Waterpipe smokers under Galata Bridge.

The City and the People

There will always be something familiar about Istanbul's famous skyline. Curving domes rise in layers, with minarets soaring upward. In the morning the city seems to drowse behind a gauzy veil, then, progressively, it emerges as the changing light draws endless colours from the buildings. The twilight shades of plum and purple are touched with flashes from spires and windows, while the Bosphorus ripples like heavy silk shot with fire. Is-

tanbul's sunsets are as celebrated as everything else in this old crossroads of history, where, quite literally, east meets west.

The city has a foot on two continents, Europe and Asia, and the mighty Bosphorus bridge spans the space in between. A walk along a fashionable shopping street, a sophisticated evening in a waterfront restaurant will convince you Istanbul is Western. Then see the crowds crossing Galata Bridge, dodge the barrow-men wheel-

Steeped in history, brushed with magic, here east meets west.

ing their carts of cucumbers and tomatoes, penetrate into the odiferous bustle of the Spice Market or the calm of a great mosque, and you will sense the presence of the Orient.

The European side of Istanbul is cleft by the Golden Horn, a cornucopia-shaped waterway which flows down from two small valleys known as the Sweet Waters of Europe. Turkish men while away the afternoon smoking water pipes in tiny cafés, musicians strum their guitars in the Passage of Flowers, water-sellers jingle by, selling their modest ware from tin cups, and horses toss their heads decorated with strings of blue beads and amulets. The occasional gypsy flouts the law to promenade his tame bear through the very centre of town, pausing to do a brief, derisory turn within hailing distance of the sparkling, plate-glass cultural centre.

Three tremendous civilizations have formed Istanbul: Roman, Byzantine and Ottoman. For a thousand years it was the intellectual centre of the Western world. The Greek origin of its present name is *eis ten polin*, "to the city". Over the centuries it has had four names: Byzantium to the Greeks when it was founded in the 7th century B.C.; Nova Roma, or New Rome, when the Emperor Constantine transferred the capital of the Roman world here; Constantinople in his honour; and finally, Istanbul.

The powerful, opulent, despotic Ottoman Turks, nomadic tribes from the confines of the Steppes, adopted Islam and, when they settled, brought the East to Istanbul. They crowned the city with minarets, implanted fountains in the market squares and raised the Mosque of Suleiman the Magnificent to rival the Christian St. Sophia, built a millennium earlier. Both count among the sublime architectural achievements of all time. Part of the Ottoman legacy is displayed in Topkapı Palace, where the famous Topkapı emeralds flicker coldly, blue and green, and the shadows of the sultans still haunt the labyrinthine harem.

Today, some 6 million people, the estimated population of Greater Istanbul, are rapidly changing the face of their metropolis. Gardens have been replaced by high-rise buildings, vine-laden alleys are giving way to office blocks, and the

The welcome is real, so is the ageless beauty of Turkish rugs.

wooden houses, which used to lean companionably together in the older quarters, are becoming rare. So, too, are their grander cousins, the summer palaces which once graced the shores of the Bosphorus. Fortunately, the drift has been caught in time. Mystery and charm survive.

Istanbul is gateway to the Turkish Republic, 97 per cent of which lies in Asia. Legend and history permeate the country. A list of Turkish "sites"

A flowery park, a frisky horse and a tempting glimpse of Asia.

reads like a logbook from the voyage of humanity. Noah's ark is thought to have come to rest on Mount Ararat. The Virgin Mary and John the Apostle are said to have lived near Ephesus on the Aegean coast, and Ephesus itself knew visitors no less renowned than Alexander the Great and St. Paul. Jason and the Argonauts rowed their way

that terminated the ten-year siege of the city. History attributes the Trojan War to economic causes, but it's a rare visitor who, knee-deep among wild flowers and scattered marble, doesn't call up the legendary image of Helen. Her loveliness put gods and men at odds, launched ships and armies, set Troy burning and laid the Trojan plain to waste. And it is said that Homer himself was born in Smyrna, today's Izmir.

But Turkey is not only history. There's sand and sea along the Aegean, nights in bougainvillea-bright restaurants, swimming, dancing and boating. Kuşadası and Çeşme offer beaches from the ultra-fashionable to the untouched. Bodrum, in the shade of its prestigious castle, is the scene for the young and affluent. Marmaris, set where the Aegean embraces the Mediterranean, basks in the heat below pine-covered hills. At Pamukkale, inland from Izmir, you can bathe among drowned Roman columns before the snowy landscape of the Cotton Castle, a series of fantastic natural lime terraces and mineral pools.

against the treacherous currents of the Bosphorus in search of the Golden Fleece. Today's oil tankers find the celebrated strait just as difficult to negotiate.

Troy is in Turkey. Look out from the walls across the windy plain. You can almost hear the clash of armour in the rustling grass. Here, according to Homer's *Iliad*, the great warriors Hector, Achilles and Ajax met their end. Here, cunning Odysseus devised the wooden horse

You can let go with clothing and behaviour in resorts, provided that elsewhere you bear in mind that this is an **11**

Islamic country, where family virtues and personal modesty win respect. On acquaintance, the apparently introverted Turk proves to be friendly, endowed with a quick sense of humour and hospitable far beyond the point of mere generosity.

Turkish cuisine excels in fresh food: hot, unleavened *pide* bread, delicious lamb, fish straight from the ocean, spiny lobsters of such gargantuan proportions that they look as though they're ready to gallop around the table. Prepare to sample melons bursting with sweetness, cherries with an aftertaste of wild almonds, little yellow loquats, the famous figs of Smyrna and, in village squares, ripe white and red mulberries, which amicable villagers are happy for you to pick.

Shopping offers bargains and authentic workmanship. Themes of love, jealousy, hope and happiness are woven into Turkey's carpets and kilims, which represent one of the summits in national art forms. Whether they're from the looms of central Anatolia or from the coast, each has a story to tell.

At the end of the day, when the lights blink on, there's oriental dancing and entertainment to equal anything in the world.

A Brief History

The Republic of Turkey is young among nations, but the country's history goes back to the dawn of humanity. Three per cent of its present area link it to Europe; the rest lies in Asia, on the Anatolian peninsula, a huge expanse of mountains and plateaus. Turkey's importance as a hinge between east and west is nothing new: it has always played this role, simply because of its situation.

Implements from the Stone Age show that Anatolia was already inhabited in the Middle Palaeolithic Period—between 100,000 and 40,000 B.C. Millennia later, some 5,000 years ago, the Bronze Age originated around the Nile and Tigris and Euphrates. Royal graves have been found in Anatolia containing bronze objects from the 3rd millennium B.C.

About this time the Sumerians of Mesopotamia (the region between the Tigris and the Euphrates in today's Iraq) developed pictographs into a cuneiform (wedge-shaped) script. Some 1,000 years later, Assyrian traders introduced this invention to Anatolia, where the indigenous Hatti people had reached an advanced intellectual level.

The Hittites

Most prosperous of all the Assyrian colonies was ancient Kanesh, today's Kültepe, near Kayseri, one of Turkey's foremost archaeological sites. Tablets from there bear evidence of increasing numbers of Hittite people moving into the area from about 1500 B.C. Their origins remain mysterious (their language was deciphered only in 1915), but they came from the direction of the Caucasus mountains. Two hundred years later they were firmly ensconced.

Hittite domination is divided into three periods: the Old Kingdom (c. 1600–1450 B.C.), the New or Empire Period (1450–1200 B.C.) and the Late Hittite Period (1200–700 B.C.). An early capital rose at Hattusa (now Boğazköy), east of Ankara. Extensive fortifications and temples were erected, as well as a citadel encompassing an impressive library of 3,350 cuneiform tablets built in the 13th century B.C.

During the momentous Empire Period, an energetic Hittite king, Muwatallis, overcame the forces of the Egyptian pharaoh, Ramses II, at Kadesh in c. 1288 B.C. Ramses never conceded defeat; he was too proud for that. He even had obelisks inscribed claiming victory. But he was sufficiently aware of Hittite strength to make terms with the next king, Hattusili III. Until about 1200 B.C., Hittites and Egyptians wielded comparable and unchallenged power.

The Hittite Empire ended with the arrival of the Phrygians and Achaeans, or "Sea Peoples", who forced the Hittites south into the mountains, where they remained until advancing Assyrians took over, this time to rule and not to trade.

Troy and After

Meanwhile, far away on the Aegean coast, other events had been taking place. The ancient Greeks traditionally recounted their history starting from the fall of Troy. Much clamorous academic discussion surrounds the exact date of the Trojan War, but it probably took place in 1240 B.C.

Strategically set above the Hellespont, now known as the Dardanelles, nine Troys rose and fell over the centuries. There is no doubt that the Trojan War did occur, although it has never been established just which of the superimposed layers of ruined cities was the actual site. Archaeologists hesitate between the levels known as Troy VIIa and Troy VI. In

Homer's accounts in the *Iliad* and the *Odyssey*, Troy was a well-organized, wealthy city, governed by the prudent, peace-loving King Priam.

Within a century, the Mycenaean Greeks who conquered Priam's city saw their own civilization decline. A race known as the Dorians either invaded or gained power in southern Greece, motivating many mainlanders to pack up their chattels and families and set forth across the Aegean to the coast of Anatolia. They immigrated in waves. First came the Aeolians, who went to the northern stretch of coastline above old Smyrna, creating a region known as Aeolis; then the Ionians, who settled south between Smyrna and the river Maeander. Smyrna itself started as an Aeolian town, then it became Ionian. Later, the Dorians followed, installing themselves south of the Maeander, in Caria.

Mainland Greece plunged into a dark age of limited achievement. Not so Ionia, where an outstanding culture evolved. Before 800 B.C. the 12 main Ionian cities banded together to form the Pan-Ionic League. Later, Smyrna was admitted as a 13th member. The arts, science and philosophy thrived. Not that everything was peaceful—the cities continued to squabble among themselves—but their citizens lived well, and many of the settlements founded colonies.

Rich as Croesus

Inland lived the Lydians, powerful and wealthy neighbours who pushed west towards the Aegean coast to set up their capital at Sardis. Croesus, the most famous Lydian king, owed his legendary fortune to gold from the River Pactolus and, according to Greek tradition, invented the first coins of standard shape and weight. Unfortunately for him, Croesus' ambitions took him east as well as west, into Persia, where he was roundly defeated. He was driven back to Sardis, only to witness the sacking of his city by Cyrus the Great in 546 B.C.

With Lydia absorbed, the Greek coastal cities lay wide open to the Persians, who lost no time incorporating them into their empire. Ionia attempted rebellion but was easily subdued in 494 B.C. Provoked by Athenian support for the Ionians, the Persian king Darius directed his attention to the Greek mainland. He was defeated at Marathon in

Ancient Rome's legacy includes the imposing library at Ephesus.

ΑΡΕΤΗ
ΚΕΛΣΟΥ

490, and ten years later his son Xerxes lost his fleet at Salamis. The following year, on the same day, Xerxes' army was defeated at Plataea and his fleet at Mycale. The coastal cities were encouraged to cluster together into the Delian Confederacy, paying tribute to Athens in return for protection against the Persians. Athens grew so attached to this easy source of income that pleas for release from the agreement went unheard. Sparta won the remunerative Confederacy from Athens at the outcome of the Peloponnesian War. The alert Persians, sensing weakness, rushed to the attack, and the Greek cities of the Aegean coast were theirs at last.

Alexander's Dream

A new star was rising on the Greek mainland: Macedon in the far north, whose king, Philip II, aimed at unifying the Greek world. His wildest dreams were fulfilled after his death by his son, Alexander the Great, in a short lifetime of 33 years. In 334 B.C., aged 24, Alexander crossed the Hellespont. He paused to pay homage to the heroes of Troy before taking over the whole Aegean coast. After conquering Syria and Egypt, he overcame Persepolis, the Persian capital, before advancing further still into India. In 12 years he established some 70 cities across the face of the eastern world. Aristotle's most brilliant pupil, Alexander dreamed of a world empire. The dream foundered. At his death the conquered territory was divided among various generals, whose antagonism and expansionist lust finally laid their land open to Roman incursions. Some of Alexander's legacy survived, notably the Greek language, which had become the usual medium for business and cultured discussions.

Enter the Romans

Outstanding among coastal cities was Pergamum, governed by the Attalid dynasty. The last Attalid king, Attalus III, has gone down in history as an odd character. One of his hobbies was inventing poisons and testing them on reluctant slaves. Just how eccentric he had become was not clear until his death (from natural causes) in 133 B.C., when Pergamese citizens were dismayed to learn he had bequeathed the whole kingdom to the Romans. Thus Pergamum became capital of the new Roman province they called Asia. Mithradates VI, king of Pontus, tried to resist Roman occupation, going so far as to order the massacre of all Romans in Asia, irrespective of age, sex or rank. This act of atrocity accounted for 80,000 lives. But the Romans got their revenge: after numerous campaigns, their troops triumphed.

In 27 B.C. Octavian took the title Augustus; Rome ceased to be a republic and became an empire. There followed a long period of calm prosperity known as the *Pax Romana* ("Roman Peace"). All Asia Minor was now incorporated into the Roman Empire. Except for the military bases where Latin was the normal means of communication, coastal citizens still spoke Greek, while Anatolian languages continued among the people who had always used them. The old Greek cities were embellished with grandiose Roman buildings, many the result of private donations.

A new religion was causing problems. Christianity represented a threat because it challenged the sanctity of the official gods and the emperor. The voyages of the Apostle Paul, from A.D. 40 to 56, removed some of the mystery that had made Christianity appear dangerous in the eyes of the establishment. As he journeyed, he set up Christian communities, notably the Asian churches addressed in the Revelation of St. John: Ephesus, Smyrna, Pergamum, Thyatira, Sardis, Philadelphia and Laodicea.

Byzantium the Golden

Byzantium had already developed on the banks of the Bosphorus and the Golden Horn. Legend claims that a Greek, Byzas, arrived in about 660 B.C. to found a settlement in obedience to the Delphic Oracle, which bade him build his city "in front of the blind". When he saw that early settlers were living in present-day Kadıköy on the Asian shore, he presumed they were the "blind", because they had overlooked the supreme appeal of the other, European bank, where he set up his town.

Byzantium, like the coastal cities, had encountered the power of Athens, Sparta, Persia and Alexander the Great. It attempted independence from Rome but was too small to hold out against the new mistress of the world and was conquered by the emperor Septimius Severus in A.D. 196. At first he punished the Byzantians with acts of destruction, then, seduced by the sheer loveliness of the place, he began to build, enlarging and strengthening the old defensive walls.

A succession of inadequate 17

rulers led to the gradual decline of the Roman Empire. In 293 Diocletian thought to strengthen it by dividing it into two parts. He became Emperor of the East, while the West was governed by Maximian. This momentous decision was to have incalculable effects. Byzantium, already renowned, stood as capital of the eastern empire. However, after the abdication of Diocletian and Maximian in 305, the empire continued to weaken, harassed by Germanic tribes. For a time, Constantine and Licinius ruled in harmony, then relations deteriorated. In 324 Constantine, who supported Christianity, defeated his pagan ally and reunited the whole empire. He immediately began construction of a new capital, choosing Byzantium as the site. It was to be known by the name Secunda

St. Saviour in Chora houses masterpieces of Byzantine art.

Roma; soon it became Nova Roma, then Constantinopolis in honour of the emperor. He officially inaugurated his city with tremendous ceremony in 330. Constantine added to the walls, following an outline suggested, he claimed, in a vision of Christ. The circuit included seven hills, in memory of the seven hills of Rome. The emperor died a confessed Christian.

In the Christian world, Constantinople achieved a pre-eminence it was to maintain for 1,000 years after the fall of Rome in 476 to the Germanic tribes. However, the city was constantly under threat of invasion, while subjected internally to endless political and religious wrangling.

The Byzantine or Eastern Roman Empire (476-1453) knew its finest hours in the 6th century under Justinian the Great. His reign produced a laudable legal system, the celebrated Code of Justinian, and saw the empire extend to Spain, Italy and Africa. Creative art was encouraged, producing rich, colourful styles in furniture and clothing, and gloriously illuminated manuscripts. As part of a great building programme, the unsurpassed basilica of St. Sophia was constructed.

After the death of the Prophet Muhammad in 632, the tremendous expansion of the Arabs led to the development of the Islamic empire. Syria, Jerusalem and Egypt were rapidly taken from the Byzantines. Constantinople was seriously threatened from 674 to 678; however its walls withstood siege. The Byzantine Empire continued to diminish with the loss of North Africa and Italy, then saw another golden age under Basil I (867-886) who greatly increased military strength. In 1042 Seljuk Turks, who had originated in central Asia, began to drive the Byzantines from Asia Minor, and the Normans won control of Sicily and Naples: the empire was slowly crumbling.

Although the Greek and Roman churches had split, western Christendom stood allegedly on the side of Byzantium when it came to confronting "infidel" races such as the Seljuk Turks. Islamized in the 10th century, the Seljuks were fiercely committed to their new religion. They overran Anatolia, menacing Christian holy places and swooping on pilgrims bound for Jerusalem. The First Crusade was organized to help the Byzantines recapture the Holy Land from the Muslims; it resulted in victory for the crusaders. During the Second and Third crusades, the European Christians suffered overwhelming defeat. The Fourth, launched in 1202, abetted by Venetian jealousy of Byzantium's merchant prowess, turned against Constantinople. The city which had held out against so many attacks was subjected to mindless pillaging by fellow Christians. The crusaders ruled the city from 1204 until 1261; they called their state Romania, which is sometimes referred to as the Latin Empire. Gold, silver, jewels and works of art were stripped from the monuments.

The Lascarid dynasty in Nicaea (Iznik) across the Bosphorus from Constantinople, a remnant of the Byzantine Empire, helped the shattered city to its feet in 1261. However, the era had reached its end: Constantinople was never the same again.

Mehmet the Conqueror

By the 15th century the Ottoman Turks, whose origins were similar to those of the Seljuks, were in control of the whole of Anatolia except Constantinople, which they coveted and frequently besieged. Nicaea's days had proved numbered. In 1330 it was taken by Orhan, first Ottoman sultan. An Ottoman capital was set up in nearby Bursa, before being moved to Edirne, ancient Adrianople. The Byzantine emperor, Manuel II (1391–1425), tried to stem the tide of events by allowing a Turkish district, mosque and tribunal within his city, and by courting Turkish goodwill with a gift of gold florins; all to no avail. The young Ottoman sultan, Mehmet II, set to work to prevent help coming to a beleaguered Constantinople by blocking the routes into the city. A fortress was erected on the European side of the Bosphorus. Then Mehmet withdrew to Edirne to wait for the spring.

The Byzantines tried to protect the Golden Horn by stretching a huge iron chain across the water. They desperately strengthened the defensive walls which had so often stood them in good stead, and watched fearfully for the inevitable. On the naval side, the Turks neatly sidestepped the ruse of the chain by dragging their ships overland on rollers, before putting them together to form a bridge for the soldiers. On May 29, 1453, the final assault was made. The last Byzantine emperor, Constantine XI,

Turkey's magnificent mosques are open to everybody.

fell in the fighting, and by noon Mehmet had control of the city. His first act was to visit Saint Sophia for prayer and to declare it a mosque. After allowing his soldiers three days' pillaging, he restored order, acting with considerable leniency and good sense. Henceforth he was to be known as Fatih (the Conqueror), and his capital was named Istanbul.

Splendour and Decline

Mehmet's empire took in most of Greece and the southern Balkans, as well as Anatolia. Under Selim, grandson of the Conqueror, expansion continued.

The most lustrous period occurred during the reign of Selim's successor, Suleiman the Magnificent (1520–1566), greatest of the sultans, known to his compatriots as the Lawgiver. Ascending the throne at age 25, he ruled for 46 years, the longest reign in Ottoman history, rendered glorious by a flowering of culture which included the building of many superb mosques by his chief architect, the remarkable Sinan.

Suleiman's army captured Belgrade in 1521. Eight years later they entered Austria to besiege Vienna (raising the siege 24 days later), then they took most of Hungary. In 1522

Rhodes fell. Muslim corsairs, including the infamous Barbarossa, helped win a part of the North African coast. By the mid-17th century, the Ottoman Empire had reached its widest limits. And they were wide indeed: the frontier extended from Batumi at the extreme east of the Black Sea, southwards to Basra in present-day Iraq. A ribbon along the Red Sea included Medina and Mecca. Egypt was in Ottoman hands and so was the whole eastern coast of the Mediterranean, including Cyprus. Greece was a long-standing possession; Crete had fallen. To the north, the empire's territories included the Crimea and an area around the Sea of Azov. Dissolution was inevitable. The process was long and painful, leaving in its wake many problems which still cause trouble in the Middle East today.

Among internal concerns was insurrection from a corps of soldiers known as the *Yeniçeri* ("new troops") or Janissaries. Originally composed of prisoners of war, they later included boys levied from Christian families and converted to the Muslim faith. Sinan himself was one. Later this type of conscription ceased; more and more the Janissaries were made

Museum tableau depicts Mehmet's entry into Constantinople.

They were not controlled until the early part of the 19th century.

up of a bunch of adventurers drawn from many races. Hated and feared throughout the land, they attained such a position of strength that they practically ran the sultanate.

The Twilight Years

The year 1821 marked the beginning of the war for Greek independence, finally achieved 11 years later. Attempts at reform within the decaying Ottoman Empire had been left too late. In any case, these reforms, albeit genuine, were interrupted by the Crimean War, in which Britain and France supported Turkey against Russia. By 1876 the government was bankrupt. The ruling sultan, Abdul Hamid II, misinterpreting the spirit of the times, tried to apply absolute rule to a country staggering under a load of debt, with a population of mutually hostile groups.

Abdul Hamid's reforms bore fruit in the end—but not in the way he had anticipated. Young army officers and the professional classes were increasingly interested in Western ideals. European literature was being widely studied. Robert College, an American school, and Galatasaray, the French *lycée* in Istanbul, were providing intelligent boys with new ideas of democracy, while Turkish girls, so long shut off from the world, were exposed to similar thoughts in the American women's college at Arnavutköy. These new intellectuals formed a group known as the Young Turks. At first the movement remained underground. Its centre was Salonica, and it was there ultimately that revolt broke out. In 1909 Abdul Hamid was deposed and replaced by Mehmet V, his brother.

There followed the Balkan Wars in which Turkey lost Macedonia and western Thrace, then World War I with Turkey on the side of Germany. In 1915, in the Gallipoli Campaign, the Turks defeated the Allied attack on the Dardanelles.

At the end of the war, the Turks had to sign the Treaty of Sèvres, which formally ended the existence of the Ottoman Empire. Greece was given large concessions, Armenia was to be an independent state; the British, French and Italians were granted the right to occupy what was left of the Turkish lands. The subsequent period of internal strife with Greeks and Armenians living in Anatolia, and struggles with occupying Entente powers was dominated by the figure of Mustafa Kemal who, from small beginnings in Macedonia, had risen to become the charismatic leader of Turkish nationalism. In 1920, with the establishment of the Turkish National Assembly, he was elected president and invested with executive power. From 1919 to 1922 he led the Turko-Greek War, which culminated in Greek defeat and withdrawal from Asia Minor. He was then faced with placating the religious elements in his government, while abolishing the sultanate. This meant deposing Sultan Mehmet VI, whose very person stood for the old ideas of combined religious and secular power. The manoeuvre was delicate. Kemal handled it with his usual vigour in a speech to the Assembly: "...it was by force that the sons of Osman seized the sovereignty... now the Turkish nation has rebelled and put a stop to these usurpers."

On November 10, 1922, the sultan, almost bereft of entourage, slipped quietly away from his palace to a waiting British warship. A caliph was appointed as religious leader, with powers strictly limited by Turkish secular law. The office was abolished in 1924.

A Modern State

In 1923 the Treaty of Lausanne defined Turkey's modern sovereignty and borders. Greece and Turkey exchanged their expatriate populations in a movement involving thousands of people.

The decade 1925–1935 witnessed the introduction of resounding reforms. Mustafa Kemal, now usually spoken of as Atatürk (Father of the Turks), set to work secularizing institutions, adapting the Latin alphabet for the Turkish language, emancipating Turkish women, changing the calendar, revising the laws and improving agriculture and industry. He did more than anyone to mould Turkey into a dependable modern nation with a belief in Western democracy. When Atatürk died in 1938, Turks in their thousands lined the track to salute the white presidential train carrying him through the night for burial in Ankara, his new capital.

Turkey remained neutral during World War II. The Democratic Party was elected to power in 1950, staying in position until 1960. The government, faced with ever-increasing economic and social difficulties, was overthrown by the Turkish Army, directed by a National Unity Committee. A new constitution consolidating modernizing reforms was approved by referendum in 1961. Social unrest led to another military coup in September 1980. A new constitution was prepared, and new legislation concerning political parties and elections was drawn up.

In 1983, Turgut Özal was elected prime minister. He is a former world banker and economist. Under his government, Turkey is aiming to achieve an industrialized Western economy.

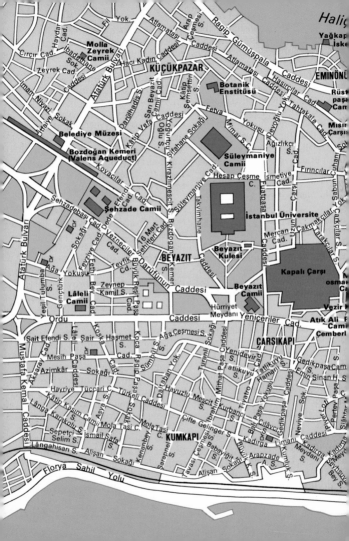

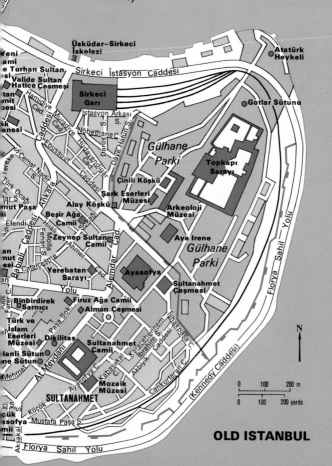

(Golden Horn)

OLD ISTANBUL

N

| 0 | 100 | 200 m |
| 0 | 100 | 200 yards |

What to See

Istanbul can easily be divided into three sections. In Europe, the Old City stretches from Seraglio Point *(Sarayburnu)* to the Theodosian Walls, 7 kilometres (4½ m.) inland, south of the Golden Horn; while the modern town, Beyoğlu, spreads up the hills north of the waterway. This is the commercial quarter and the main hotel and shopping district. On the Asian bank of the Bosphorus, Scutari *(Üsküdar)* is mainly a residential area.

In the Old City, the greatest concentration of major sites lies in Sultanahmet: the Blue Mosque, Saint Sophia and the Yerebatan Cistern are close to the Hippodrome Square, while Topkapı Palace and the Archaeological Museum are within easy walking distance. The central area, which can be covered enjoyably on foot, contains the Grand Bazaar and the Mosque of Suleiman.

It's probably best to select individually from the remaining monuments on the southern shore of the Golden Horn and use transport to visit them.

There are plenty of buses and communal taxis *(dolmuş)*; ordinary taxis are metered and fairly inexpensive. Our itinerary for this section starts at the Valens Aqueduct and winds to the former church of St. Saviour in Chora, second only to St. Sophia as a Byzantine masterpiece.

As a summary of sights and sounds, take time to wander the picturesque Eminönü district and the little streets at the back of the Spice Market.

Istanbul's mighty Bosphorus bridge links Europe to Asia.

You'll certainly want to take a boat trip along the Bosphorus, zig-zagging from one palace, fortress or little town to another, almost as far as the Black Sea. Dolmabahçe Palace, Yıldız Park and Rumeli Hisarı are all situated along the European shore of the Bosphorus. The Asian shore is the site of Beylerbeyi Palace, Çamlıca Park and Anadolu Hisarı. You can make a similar excursion along the Golden Horn to Eyüp, one of the holiest places in the Muslim world. The Princes' Islands in the Sea of Marmara are also interesting to visit. Normal ferries serve all these places.

Because of its exceptional interest, we have included Bursa as an excursion from Istanbul, even though it necessitates an overnight stay. As a contrast to Istanbul, try to visit the Aegean coast for fascinating ancient sites as well as sea and sand. The area is described in a separate section.

Old Istanbul

If you are staying in the hotel district, you will have to cross the Galata Bridge to reach the Old City. From the bridge you catch a glimpse of the Asian shore and Leander's Tower, a lighthouse sitting off the coast in the Sea of Marmara. The New Mosque stands in a square where the bridge ends. To the right you can see the imposing mass of the Mosque of Suleiman the Magnificent, seemingly etched against the hillside. In the opposite direction are the roofs of Topkapı Palace and the dome of St. Sophia, which will prove invaluable landmarks, as will the six minarets of the Blue Mosque, needling upwards right alongside the vast, open area of the Hippodrome.

Sultanahmet District

The spacious square known as *At Meydani* ("Square of Horses") gives only a faint idea of the magnificence of the **Hippodrome** in Byzantine times, when it was central to the city's life. Inspired by the Circus Maximus in Rome, it was designed as a stadium for chariot racing and public activities. First built in 203, and enlarged by Constantine the Great, the Hippodrome finally attained tremendous dimensions—approximately 400 metres long by 120 across (1,300 by 400 ft.) —and provided seating for 100,000 people.

The Hippodrome was the scene of the official ceremony founding the city of New Rome in 330. Today, few signs remain of past pageantry, for the Hippodrome was destroyed during the Fourth Crusade and gradually stripped of everything, even its marble seats. Statues were melted down for coins. In the 17th century the ruins were quarried to help build the Blue Mosque.

The entrance to the central axis, or *spina*, is marked by a fountain in a helmet-shaped edifice with an ornate gilt and mosaic ceiling, given by Kaiser Wilhelm II to mark his visit to the city in 1900. Three ancient monuments survive along the *spina* itself.

The **Egyptian Obelisk** was commissioned by Thutmose III (1549–1503 B.C.). Brought here in A.D. 390 by the Emperor Theodosius, this is only the top of the original column. Perfectly preserved hieroglyphics inscribed on the smooth pink granite record that Thutmose raised the monument in honour of the Egyptian sun god, Amon Re, and to commemorate his own military

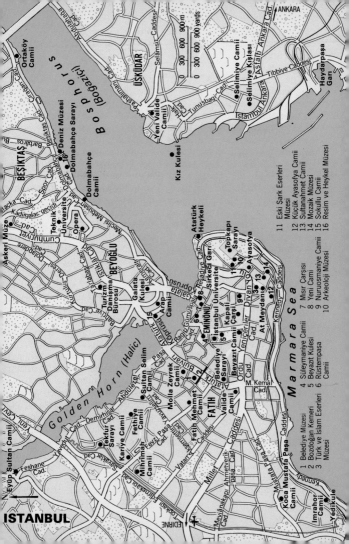

ISTANBUL

Bosphorus (İçi)

ANKARA

ÜSKÜDAR

BEŞİKTAŞ

BEYOĞLU

EMİNÖNÜ

FATİH

Golden Horn (Haliç)

Marmara Sea

11 Eski Sark Eserleri
   Müzesi
12 Küçük Ayasofya Camii
13 Sultanahmet Camii
14 Mozaik Müzesi
15 Sokullu Camii
16 Resim ve Heykel Müzesi

1 Belediye Müzesi
2 Bozdoğan Kemeri
3 Türk ve İslam Eserleri
   Müzesi

4 Süleymaniye Camii
5 Beyazıt Kulesi
6 Rüstempaşa
   Camii

7 Mısır Carşısı
8 Yeni Cami
9 Nuruosmaniye Camii
10 Arkeoloji Müzesi

Ortaköy Camii
Deniz Müzesi
Dolmabahçe Sarayı
Dolmabahçe Camii
Kız Kulesi
Yeni Valide Camii
Selimiye Camii
Selimiye Kışlası
Haydarpaşa Garı
Atatürk Heykeli
Topkapı Sarayı
Ayasofya
Galata Kulesi
Arap Camii
Türizm Danışma Bürosu
Opera
Üniversite
Teknik Üniversite
Askeri Müze
İstanbul Üniversite
At Meydanı
Sultan Selim
Molla Zeyrek Camii
Zeyrek Camii
Belediye Sarayı
Fatih Mehmet Camii
Valide
Fethiye Camii
Kariye Camii
Mihrimah Camii
Tekfur Sarayı
Feshane Cad.
Eyüp Sultan Camii
Koca Mustafa Paşa Camii
İmrahor Camii
Yedikule

300 600 900 m
300 600 900 yards

conquests. Bas-reliefs on the Byzantine base depict Theodosius and his family in different scenes.

The **Serpentine Column**, originally in the form of three bronze snakes wound together to support a gold vase, is the oldest Greek monument in Istanbul. Constantine the Great brought it from Delphi, where it commemorated the Greek victory over the Persians at Plataea in 479 B.C.

A second obelisk, of indeterminate date, is known as the **Column of Constantine Porphyrogenitus**, because a Greek inscription on its base records that the Emperor Constantine VII Porphyrogenitus (913–959) restored and covered it with gilded bronze plates.

On the western side of the Hippodrome, don't miss the **Turkish and Islamic Arts Museum** *(Türk ve İslam Eserleri Müzesi)*. The collection is housed in **İbrahim Paşa Sarayı**, the palace of Suleiman's son-in-law, recently reopened after extensive renovation. Apart from superlative illuminated Korans, Turkish and Persian miniatures, carpets and faïence, you'll also see utilitarian objects, giving insight into Turko-Islamic life from the 8th century to the present day.

Blue Mosque

Known in Turkish as *Sultan Ahmet Camii*, this graceful mosque lends its name to the whole surrounding district. It was designed in the early 17th century by the architect Mehmet Ağa, spoken of during his lifetime as *Sedefkâr* ("worker in mother-of-pearl").

The mosque rises from the ground in sensuously undulating domes and half-domes, with six slender minarets shooting skyward.

Inside, everything seems to float in the azure light reflected from the blue tiles which give the mosque its name. There are 21,043 ceramic tiles from the town of Iznik, celebrated for the tile industry since the mid-15th century. Lilies, carnations, tulips and roses bloom in ageless, stylized beauty, glowing in the light falling from 260 windows. Until the 18th century they contained stained glass, enhancing the cerulean hues of the interior.

Four massive fluted pillars support a central cupola of gigantic proportions: 22.4 metres (70 ft.) in diameter and 43 metres (142 ft.) at the highest point.

St. Sophia's dome has awed visitors for almost 1,500 years.

The *mihrab*, or niche, placed in all mosques to show the direction of Mecca, is white marble, and so is the delicately chiselled pulpit. Inlay of ivory and mother-of-pearl enhances the ebony shutters. Painted arabesques around the upper windows are restorations, but if you're allowed under the sultan's loge, note the original decoration of marvellously swirling tendrils executed in jewel-like colours.

Before you visit St. Sophia opposite, it is worth making a short diversion to the nearby **Mosque of Sokullu Mehmet Pasha** *(Mehmet Paşa Camii),* one of the masterpieces of the greatest of all Ottoman architects, Sinan. A further example of original painted decoration, above the entrance, and fine Iznik tiles contribute to its charms.

Further downhill, towards the Sea of Marmara, stands the Byzantine church of SS. Sergius and Bacchus, known to the Turks as **Küçük Ayasofya Camii** ("Little Saint Sophia Mosque"). Some of the lacy capitals in this 6th-century building carry monograms of Justinian and his wife, Theodora, and there is a carved inscription in the gallery mentioning the royal couple and St. Sergius.

St. Sophia *(Ayasofya)*
Opposite the Blue Mosque lies the former church of St. Sophia, undisputed sovereign of Istanbul's First Hill. Constantine the Great is reputed to have built a basilica here in 325 on the site of a pagan temple. Destroyed twice by fire, it was rebuilt from 532 to 537 by the Emperor Justinian, who dedicated it to the Holy Wisdom of God (in Greek, *Hagia Sophia*).

It is one of the most remarkable buildings ever erected anywhere. The finest materials known went into its construction: special light bricks from Rhodes for the enormous cupola, red porphyry columns from Rome, silver and gold work from Ephesus, verd antique from Thessaly, white marble from the islands of Marmara and yellow marble from Africa. Four acres of the interior were covered by glowing mosaics, in which gold predominated. The whole was like a vast jewel, lit by silver candelabra.

The dome was soon damaged by earthquake, and reinforcement has coarsened the outward appearance. Supporting buttresses were put in place in the 14th century. The minarets were added after the Turkish Conquest of 1453, when St. Sophia was converted into a mosque. Sinan strengthened the buttresses in the 16th century, and the most recent restoration was carried out in the middle years of the last century. In 1935 Atatürk proclaimed St. Sophia a museum.

Visitors enter by a side door, passing through the vestibule to the inner narthex. This opens through nine doorways into the nave, a space of dramatically lofty proportions topped by the stupendous **cupola,** approximately 31 metres (100 ft.) in diameter and 55 metres (180 ft.) high. Earthquakes and restoration have squeezed it into a less than perfect circle. Arabic calligraphy around the apex of the dome was placed there after restoration in 1847, complementing panels inscribed in Arabic with Islamic holy names.

St. Sophia was a church for about 1,000 years, a mosque for 500. The Crusaders were responsible for plundering its treasures and divesting it of its glory. Mehmet the Conqueror's first act on taking Constantinople was to visit Saint Sophia, and the first ritual prayers of the new ruler were performed here.

The apse contains one of the finest **mosaics:** the Virgin Mary holding the infant Jesus, with a striking figure of the Archangel Gabriel on the supporting arch. His companion archangel, Michael, has vanished, but for a few feathers from his wings. Mount the sloping corridors leading from the narthex to the galleries for other examples. Opposite the Deesis, an extraordinary 13th-century mosaic showing Jesus flanked by the Virgin and St. John the Baptist, is the empty tomb of Enrico Dandolo, Doge of Venice, the man most responsible for the mindless pillaging of Constantinople in 1204. Several other mosaics show emperors and empresses presenting gifts to the Holy Mother and Child.

Before leaving, pay a visit to the **Weeping Column** with a thumb-sized hole which remains perpetually damp because of water absorption from subterranean level. Christian legend says it's the impression of St. Gregory's finger; Muslims claim it's the spot where a holy man inserted his finger to try to turn the building towards Mecca.

Underground Palace

What about a change of focus with a visit to a cistern? Not just any cistern. This is fascinating **Yerebatan Sarayı** (Sunken Palace), a stone's throw from the Hippodrome. You descend to a vast, man-made cavern, given its name in **35** the 6th century when Justinian enlarged the original cistern built by Constantine the Great. Yerebatan Sarayı is the most famous of many water storage tanks in Istanbul. Water from the Belgrade Forest, north of Istanbul, was held here for use if the city were besieged. The 336 Byzantine columns with Corinthian capitals and the brick arches are still securely in place, reflected in dark water which stretches out of sight in a hushed twilight, 14 centuries old.

Topkapı throbs to memories of royal pomp and endless intrigue.

Topkapı Palace

Ancient residence of the Ottoman sultans, *Topkapı Sarayı* was built by Mehmet the Conqueror in 1462. Every succeeding sultan added something to the palace, which gradually became a royal city comprising mosques, bath-houses, mint, schools, libraries, residences, gardens and fountains, built around four main courtyards.

Close to the outer entrance to Topkapı is a particularly graceful **fountain** erected in the early 18th century by Ahmet III. Exquisite fountains proliferate in Turkey, where a gift of clear water to the populace is a traditional charitable gesture.

The First Court is entered through the Imperial Gate *(Bab-ı Hümayun)*, built in 1478. Then come gardens, lawns and sweeping trees, providing the right dreamlike atmosphere for penetrating further into the mysterious universe of the sultans. This area is known as the **Court of the Janissaries** after the military corps which once assembled here. Nothing remains of the former palace services such as bakeries and buildings for storing firewood; nevertheless the First Court has a treasure: the old church of St. Irene. Postpone your visit for now and continue to the fortified Gate of Salutations *(Bab-üs Selam)*. The building where the ticket office is housed occasionally served as a prison; the executioner cleaned up and rinsed his sword in the nearby fountain after a beheading. No one but the Sultan could pass through the gate on horseback, and it is still the point where all cars and taxis have to stop. It leads to the Court of the Divan, where the imperial council met, the beginning of the palace proper.

To the right of the gate lie the enormous **kitchens** built by Mehmet the Conqueror and Beyazıt II in the 15th century, considerably enlarged since then. Apart from cooking

areas, there were mosques, baths and dormitories for the various chefs, pastry-makers and scullions.

Today the kitchens house a priceless collection of **Chinese porcelain** as well as European crystal and porcelain, Ottoman cooking implements and serving dishes. There are 10,512 pieces of Chinese porcelain alone at Topkapı, of which the majority has to be kept in storage.

But this is only a start to the **37**

palace treasures. If nothing else, you must visit the **harem**. In origin the word means "sacred" or "set apart". The sultan, his mother, wives (of whom he was allowed four) and innumerable concubines all lived in this dim network of staircases, corridors, bedrooms and bathrooms, in a stifling world of ambitious intrigue. The main preoccupation of the womenfolk was to produce a male child, and then to assure his accession to the throne. It was a claustrophobic, unnatural world of jealousy and unhappiness; you may sense the troubled atmosphere lingering in the dusty sunlight and complicated decor.

Apart from the sultan, the only adult males allowed in the harem were the black eunuchs who guarded it. You pass through the carriage gate, the exit used by the women on their rare outings, to the **black eunuchs' dormitory**. The sticks on the wall were used to beat the guilty—and the innocent—with strokes on the soles of the feet, a mandatory punishment regularly applied to all novices.

The sultan's mother, or *valide sultan*, held unique power over her son, the empire and especially the harem. Her apartments occupy most of the building west of the Courtyard

of the Valide Sultan. The bedplace with its gilded canopy is faced with 17th-century flowered tiles. The small prayerroom alongside shows scenes from Mecca and Medina.

The **Baths of the Sultan** comprise a dressing room, a cool room and the baths themselves. The sultan was bathed by elderly female servants, then attended by groups of younger handmaids wearing stilted clogs of the type still seen in Turkish antique shops, although here

The harem: exquisite setting for tales of love and sorrow.

they were most often sheathed with beaten silver.

Pass into the luxuriant **Hall of the Sultan**, with three handsome marble fountains and the canopied throne from which the sultan would watch dancing, listen to music or enjoy plays or puppet shows. The mother sultana and official wives sat on the raised platform while the more musically talented slave-girls performed from the balcony.

The suite of rooms known as the **Kiosk of Murat III** is the most amazing of all, boasting inlaid floors, flowered Iznik tiles of the best period, carved fountains and fireplaces, with a superb dome in the main chamber attributed to Sinan; the ensemble forming the epitome of 16th-century Turkish design. Don't miss the small Library (early 17th century), **39**

Secrets of the Harem

The mother, sisters and daughters of the sultan were honoured with the title Sultana, but the sultan's mother (*valide sultan)* was undisputed queen of the harem. This elite group enjoyed a modicum of freedom and could be driven around the city in closed carriages, watched over by a retinue of eunuchs. Eventually husbands were found for the younger women, and they left for their own households.

Next in importance were the sultan's four wives, or *kadın*, former favourite concubines who had been fortunate enough to have a male child. Their main aim in life was to become First Wife, and eventually rule as *valide sultan*.

Immediately a girl attracted some sign of interest from the sultan, she was given the title *gözde* (Favourite), accorded slaves and a private room, and could concentrate her wiles on being invited to the royal bedchamber, the first step to power. Once she succeeded, she was known as an *ikbal*, and if she bore a child, she became a *haseki*. But there was plenty of competition from the *cariye*, general handmaidens of the lowest rank, more than eager for a glance from their master.

They were chosen from all over the empire and carefully trained in protocol, music, dancing, the Turkish language and the Muslim religion. Many were Circassian, especially sought after for their beauty and fair skin.

On one occasion, men were permitted to see the ladies of the seraglio—but by then the empire was at an end. When Abdul Hamid was deposed in 1909 the harem was closed down, but no one knew what to do with the women. Finally their families were notified and all 213 members of the harem were assembled at Topkapı for one of the strangest identification parades ever. Rough peasants and silken-clad girls clung together as fathers claimed daughters, and brothers recognized long-lost sisters. But some women could no longer speak their native languages, others were disappointed because no one came to claim them.

In 1970 the last survivor of this pathetic group was still living in a small house in the Princes' Islands. She was rarely seen by the other residents; when she did leave the house she was heavily veiled. No one ever saw her face. No one knew her name. She was spoken of only as *Saraylı Hanım*, "the Lady of the Palace".

and the Fruit Room (early 18th century) painted in European rococo style with flowers and fruit for Ahmet III, the "Tulip King", who greeted spring every year with a tulip festival in the palace grounds.

Gold glistens in abundance in the **Treasury**, where the display starts modestly enough with a bowl of apple-green peridots, then explodes into wild magnificence: you can gaze at a pair of solid gold candlesticks, each encrusted with 666 diamonds (representing the 666 verses of the Koran); a golden throne studded with over 900 peridots; a silver-gilt cradle decorated with pearls, in which new-born princes and princesses were presented to the sultan; another throne, gold plate over wood, ornamented with enamel and precious stones. Stars of the collection are an 86-carat diamond surrounded by 49 smaller stones, known as the Spoonmaker's Diamond, displayed in the fourth hall of the Treasury and, of course, presented with suitable bravura in the second hall, the dagger rendered famous by the film, *Topkapi*. The handle contains three huge emeralds winking green fire, with a fourth on top serving as cover to a watch embedded in the hilt. The gold sheath is set with diamonds.

St. Irene
Back in Topkapı's First Court, the **Church of St. Irene** *(Aya İrini Kilisesi)* awaits a visit. It was built by Justinian in the form of a domed basilica, more or less at the same time as St. Sophia. The name means "divine peace", which did nothing to dissuade the Janissaries from using it as an arms depot. Recently the church has undergone restoration, and concerts are held here, especially during the Istanbul Festival in June.

Museums
Three exceptional museums are placed conveniently next to one another in a nearby courtyard. Even if you're not a history-lover, don't miss the **Archaeological Museum** *(Arkeoloji Müzesi)*. It's one of the most famous in the world, especially reputed for its collection of sarcophagi.

The **Museum of the Ancient Orient** *(Eski Şark Eserleri Müzesi)* displays a rich collection of objects from ancient Near and Middle Eastern civilizations. Among them figure Babylonian panels from the time of King Nebuchadnezzar (605–562 B.C.), enigmatically smiling statuettes from Mesopotamia and clay tablets bearing Hammurabi's law code in cuneiform lettering. **41**

The most eye-catching building in this square, the **Tiled Kiosk** *(Çinili Köşkü)*, built by Mehmet the Conqueror in 1472, was designed as a hunting lodge and has remained practically unchanged. The exterior tiles are mostly from the Seljuk period. Inside is a valuable display of ceramics from Seljuk times to the 20th century.

Central District

A broad, straight road, Divan Yolu, runs all the way from Sultan Ahmet Square to Beyazıt Square, the most animated area of the old city, set on the Third Hill. It was a main street in Byzantine times, just as it is today. On the right, almost midway along, rises the **Burnt Column**, charred by a great fire which raged here in 1770. Constantine erected it in May 330 to mark the city's new status as capital of the Roman Empire. As well as pagan relics, nails from the Cross on which Christ was crucified and part of the Cross itself were reputed to be sealed in the base.

Behind the Burnt Column, the Baroque exterior of **Nuruosmaniye Camii** (1755) contrasts with the simplicity of the interior, where 174 windows reflect the meaning of the name of the mosque: "Light of Osman".

Beyazıt Square and Mosque
Pigeons wheel over the crowds in **Beyazıt Meydanı** as they have throughout the 1,600 years of its existence. Theodosius I had the square laid out in the 4th century, adding a triumphal arch in his own name as a nice finishing touch. Hefty fragments can be seen off the south-west corner.

The noble **mosque** which dominates the north-east side was built by Sultan Beyazıt, son of Mehmet the Conqueror, in the very early years of the 16th century. This peace-loving mystic, in every way the antithesis of his energetic father, thereby became responsible for the beginning of classical Ottoman architecture, drawing inspiration directly from St. Sophia. The buildings which once formed part of the mosque complex—schools, inn and public baths—are now mostly converted to other uses.

Take a moment's breather under the ancient dappled plane tree in the tea garden between the mosque and the university to observe Istanbul's student life, before you enter the Grand Bazaar. The

Istanbul's university stands alongside wide Beyazıt square.

Beyazıt Tower, looming in the university grounds beyond the big monumental gates, was a fire lookout, placed there in 1828. Athletic visitors can climb 179 steps for a memorable panoramic view.

Grand Bazaar

Covered market, *Kapalı Çarşı*— call it what you will, the Grand Bazaar looks like Ali Baba's cave and sounds like the trading post for the Tower of Babel. This is the biggest oriental market in the world. It's like a complete city, with a many-domed roof. There are quiet alleys, lively crossroads and main streets.

Mehmet the Conqueror had a covered market built on the site in 1461. It has been reconstructed several times after destruction by fire and earthquake. Nowadays it contains about 4,000 shops, as well as banks, cafés, restaurants and mosques. The most ancient part is the Old Bedesten at the

centre, kept for more valuable merchandise since it can be securely locked at night.

Even if you've no intention of buying anything, visit the Covered Market for a distillation of Istanbul and Turkey. It's a kaleidoscope of constantly-changing brilliance. Voices call out in a dozen languages. Water-sellers come jangling by; incredibly strong men, *hamal,* lumber past, harnessed into a kind of leather saddle and transporting anything up to a sofa and chairs on their backs.

Afterwards, the **Book Market** *(Sahaflar Çarşısı)* comes as a much-needed respite. There are works in every language. You're quite likely to find a gorgeously illuminated Koran not far from a copy of Plato's *Republic*, or a faded photograph of Sinatra propped up on a well-thumbed copy of Donald Duck.

Mosque of Suleiman the Magnificent

Sober in outline, harmonious in its classic proportions, the *Süleymaniye* is beautifully positioned above the Golden Horn, a tribute to two men of genius, Suleiman, the sultan who saw the Ottoman Empire to the zenith of its power, and Sinan, his chief architect. The mosque was built between 1550 and 1557 by some 5,300 workmen.

You enter through a broad courtyard with a rectangular marble and gilt bronze ablutions fountain. Daylight floods into the interior through 16th-century stained glass windows. The dome is 53 metres (175 ft.) high, the interior of the mosque itself measures 57 by 60 metres (187 by 197 ft.). Four porphyry columns mark its corners. Iznik tiles are set either side of the *mihrab*. Doors and shutters are fastidiously worked with ivory and mother-of-pearl.

According to legend, jewels from Persia were mixed with the cement for the buildings and the incredible acoustics were attained by embedding 64 hollow jars neck-down in the dome. Try making the slightest sound at the base of one of the pillars and you'll hear it amplified and repeated in echoes. It's said, too, that Suleiman recognized greatness when he saw it: he gave the keys of the mosque to Sinan, and it was the architect, not the sultan, who opened it.

Suleiman the Magnificent, also called "the Great" and "the Lawgiver", reigned for 46 years from his accession in 1520. During this golden age, the arts and sciences flourished. The Süleymaniye is considered the finest of all the mosques in Istanbul for the harmony of its domes, cupolas and arcades.

Both the sultan and the architect (who was almost 100 when he died) are buried in the grounds. Take time for a stroll there. When in season, irises, roses and mauve hollyhocks tangle in long grass between leaning gravestones, while sparrows swoop and squabble in the fig trees. Sinan lies in a modest mausoleum on the periphery of the grounds, while Suleiman has a far grander tomb, decorated with Iznik tiles and original painting, the imperial turban at his head. The tomb of Süleiman's wife Roxelana is also decorated with magnificent Iznik tiles.

Walking around the terrace, which affords a superb view towards the Galata Bridge, you'll be aware of the immensity of the whole complex, which included bath-houses, schools, caravanserai, a library, kitchens, a refuge for the poor and houses for attendants. You'll also be able to note the minarets: two with two balconies, the other two with three. Four minarets signify that Suleiman was the fourth sultan to reign in Istanbul; the total of ten balconies indicates that he was the tenth monarch to lead the Ottoman Empire.

Outer City

There's a whole garland of mosques and Byzantine churches looping through this neighbourhood, which becomes more picturesque as you work your way towards St. Saviour in Chora and down to the Balat and Fener districts along the Golden Horn. Anatolian families moving to Istanbul add colour to old districts, where you have to pick your way over cobbles and the occasional unpaved rocky track between tottering wooden houses strung with washing. You may even be a bit of a curiosity yourself, but the interest will be friendly.

Start at Şehzadebaşı Caddesi. The imposing **Mosque of the Prince** *(Şehzade Camii)* is one of Sinan's early works, completed in 1548. It was constructed as a memorial for Suleiman the Magnificent's son, Prince Mehmet, who died in 1543 at the age of 21.

From there, strutting in fine style across Atatürk Bulvarı, are the remains of the **Valens Aqueduct** *(Bozdoğan Kemeri)*, whose pedigree goes back to the 2nd century. The Emperor Valens had it rebuilt in the 4th century; it has been restored several times since, and was still in use during the last century. In its heyday the aqueduct supplied water to a central cistern, **45** first for the Byzantine palace, later for Topkapı. You can sit below the arches in the garden courtyard of a serene, 16th-century building, now the **Municipal Museum** *(Belediye Müzesi)*, which is worth a visit for paintings of old Istanbul and a dusty but endearing clutter of photographs, costumes, glassware, writing effects and assorted memorabilia.

Mehmet the Conqueror and his family are buried in the grounds of **Fatih Camii**, built on the Fourth Hill between 1462 and 1470, but reconstructed after an earthquake in 1766. The extensive complex, biggest in the whole Ottoman Empire, included a hospital, a mental asylum, poorhouses, and accommodation for visitors, irrespective of race and religion. Numerous schools taught science, mathematics and history as well as religious law. At the time, such enlightened philanthropy and education were unusual anywhere in the world.

Take Yavuz Selim Caddesi for a view of fig trees, apple trees, neat vegetable patches and the red-tiled roofs of little houses, all planted below the road and surrounded by the remains of Roman walls, in front of the Mosque of Selim I. This pretty village occupies the dried-out **Cistern of Aspar**, and is known in Turkish as *Çukurbostan* (Sunken Garden).

Dominating the Fifth Hill, the **Mosque of Selim I** *(Sultan Selim Camii)* is dedicated to Suleiman the Magnificent's father. Pass through the colourful courtyard to look out over the sluggish waters of the

Golden Horn, and you'll catch sight of St. George's, the Greek Orthodox Patriarchate. Below is the district of Fener and further up the Golden Horn is Balat. To wander through these narrow streets is to witness another Istanbul. Sit on a doorstep (no one will mind) and watch the children play-

ing old and strangely familiar street-games, while their mothers, clad in vivid trousers and modest headscarves, and their grandmothers, swathed in black, chat in groups, pausing

Time has only mellowed the ancient brickwork of St. Saviour.

for a glance or a shy smile in your direction.

Chickens squawk in the courtyard of the **Church of Theotokos Pammakaristos** *(Fethiye Camii),* and washing flaps among piles of masonry. One part of the building is retained for Christian worship, the other is a mosque. Examine what remains of the series of 14th-century mosaics which once adorned the church.

One of the brightest jewels in Istanbul's Byzantine crown is the former church of St. Saviour in Chora, **Kariye Camii,** now a museum containing outstanding frescoes and mosaics. When the church was built it stood outside the city walls, justifying the Greek name *Chora,* meaning "countryside".

The oldest part is the central domed area, dated 1120. The church was rebuilt early in the 14th century by Theodore Metochites, statesman, scholar and art-lover, close friend and advisor to the Emperor Andronicus II Palaeologus. Sadly, this cultured humanist was reduced to poverty when the emperor was overthrown and saw out the last years of his life in Chora monastery among the glorious works of art with which he had embellished it. He outlived Andronicus by only one month.

Metochites left the central structure untouched but probably added the outer narthex and the parecclesion or sidechapel. The church was converted into a mosque in 1511 but was not altered, apart from the addition of a minaret and the sealing up of some windows. Wooden screens were placed over the **mosaics**. These are usually grouped into six categories and depict the life of Jesus and the Virgin Mary. The mosaic over the door leading into the nave has a likeness of Metochites presenting his beloved church to Christ. To intensify the effect of light, each tile was set at a slightly different depth and angle, creating a shimmering, moving surface.

All the **frescoes** are in the parecclesion, which stretches the whole length of the building and was used in Byzantine times as a funerary chapel. There, in the semi-dome of the apse, is the masterly Resurrection *(Anastasis).*

The mosaics and frescoes may be by the same artist and are contemporaneous with Giotto's work in Padua, dating from 1310–1320. They are sometimes attributed to the Greek, Theophanes. Subtlety of colour, liveliness of posture and the strong, lifelike faces of the subjects all attest to a last extraordinary flowering of Byzantine art before its descent into decadence.

Marking the Sixth Hill is **Mihrimah Camii**, built by Sinan in 1565 for one of Suleiman's daughters. Further north lies an old palace, **Tekfur Sarayı**, part of the last major residence of the Byzantine imperial family.

Mehmet the Conqueror entered the city through the **Adrianople Gate** *(Edirnekapı)* in the **Theodosian Walls**, which were originally constructed in the 5th century. At their grandest they stretched for 17 kilometres (12 m.) from the Sea of Marmara to the Golden Horn, were fortified by 400 towers and had 50 gates of which 7 remain in use. Much of the inner wall and many of the towers are still standing.

Camping among the rubble of the proud old ramparts are Istanbul's gypsies. They have been there off and on since the 13th century when emperor Andronicus Comnenus gave them the right to set up a shantytown, known today as Sulukule.

At the Marmara end of the Theodosian Walls, a long way from the other sites of Istanbul but easily reached by the coast road, stands the ancient fortress known as **Seven Towers** *(Yedikule)*. The four Byzantine and three Turkish towers were enclosed within walls by Mehmet the Conqueror in 1470. The nearby **Golden Gate** *(Altınkapı)* existed before the construction of the city walls and was heavily decorated with marble reliefs and gold inscriptions. It was the magnificent triumphal arch of the Byzantine emperors.

Eminönü

Leave yourself the time for a leisurely walk through the district of Eminönü, where the Galata Bridge meets the south bank of the Golden Horn. Here the crowds seem at their most frenetic, the babble of voices the loudest, the odours and colours the strongest, for Eminönü is the synopsis of all the sights, sounds and smells of old Istanbul.

The square before the **New Mosque** *(Yeni Cami or Valide Camii)*, is a congregating spot for some of Istanbul's better established beggars and pedlars who have set themselves up semi-permanently in front of the 17th-century building. Seated among them, dozing in the sun, are the grain-sellers from whom, for a few liras, you can buy a cupful of seed to minister to the pigeon population.

Begun by Mehmet III's mother in 1597, the New Mosque was completed 66 years later by the mother of Mehmet IV. It contains spectacular tiles, especially in the royal gallery, reached by a separate staircase. The Egyptian or **Spice Market** *(Mısır Çarşısı)* just alongside, so-named because for centuries it has sold herbs and spices, was set up to raise money for repairs to the mosque complex.

The air is heady with the scent of ginger, pepper, saffron, eucalyptus, jasmine, incense, cinnamon, nutmeg, rosewater and freshly roasted coffee beans. In the past, the sellers used to sit cross-legged on carpets, ready to seize pestle and mortar for pounding potions both efficacious and fanciful, optimistically prepared to cure anything from lumbago to

The Spice Market draws crowds to the old Eminönü district.

love sickness, from simple cases of sore throats to highly complicated cases of combating the Evil Eye. Nor were they all charlatans. Some of the market's herbal remedies are still available, even though they no longer contain such rare ingredients as ambergris, dragon's blood and tortoise eggs.

More mundane merchandise is available, too, for the Spice Market is a popular shopping complex for anything anyone could need. Fish, flowers, clothing, secondhand shoes, wire netting, an astonishing selection of plastic buckets: all these and more are sold in the nearby streets. You can even have your spectacles repaired on the spot.

Take time out in the **Mosque of Rüstem Pasha** (*Rüstempaşa Camii*) whose minaret soars over Hasırcılar Caddesi. Another of Sinan's masterpieces, it glows inside and out with fine Iznik tiles.

Work your way along Ha-

Turkish Folk Medicine

The intelligent and cultivated Lady Mary Wortley Montagu, wife of the British Ambassador to the Ottoman Government from 1716–1718, was instrumental in introducing inoculation against smallpox to the Western world. Lady Mary described this successful example of "like curing like" (which Turkish folk healers still practise to this day) in a letter written to a friend:

"There is a set of old women who make it their business to perform the operation every autumn, in the month of September, when the great heat is abated." She goes on to describe how families grouped together so that some 15 or 16 people could be immunized at the same time: "...the old woman comes with a nutshell full of the matter of the best sort of smallpox, and asks what vein you please to have opened. She immediately rips open that you offer her with a large needle, which gives you no more pain than a common scratch, and puts into the vein as much matter as can lie upon the head of her needle and, after that, binds up the little wound with a hollow bit of shell..." The result, as with today's vaccination, was a mild fever. Lady Mary, highly impressed, continues: "There is no example of anyone that has died in it; and you may believe I am well satisfied of the safety of this experiment, since I intend trying it on my dear little son. I am patriot enough to take pains to bring this useful invention into fashion in England..."

That she set out staunchly to do. And nowadays, thanks to vaccination, the disfiguring and often deadly disease has practically disappeared.

midiye Caddesi to **Sirkeci Railway Station**, erstwhile terminus for the famous Orient Express. Then, to catch the full flavour of the district, join the crowds and walk the **Galata Bridge**, pausing first to descend underneath and explore the dozens of little fish restaurants and coffee shops, where Turkish men puff euphorically at their water pipes, staring out over the indefatigable water-traffic of the Golden Horn.

The first bridge at this point was built in 1845 by Abdul Mecit's mother. The existing structure, built in 1912 with German know-how, floats on pontoons; the central section is

Under Galata Bridge. Fresh fish in unforgettable surroundings.

opened every morning for an hour to allow tall ships to pass through.

As you cross towards the northern bank you'll see, straight ahead, rising from the district that used to be called Galata and is now Karaköy, the unmistakable outline of the Galata Tower.

Modern Istanbul

Galata and Pera

Names may change and districts lose their character, but Galata still clings to the remnants of its rip-roaring reputation, and will do so as long as there's a handful of true Galatiotes left to remember it.

Some time during the 11th century, a rough bunch of cast-off seamen and dubious drifters from every port in Europe and Asia settled along the edge of the Horn in the maritime quarter which became known as Galata. Genoese merchants had already taken up residence in the hills above the port, gradually establishing a fortified city within a city, calling themselves the Magnificent Community of Pera.

The **Galata Tower**, erected to defend this autonomous colony, is of uncertain date. It seems to have been built in 1349 in its present form, as a stronghold in the city walls. Architecturally of limited interest, the view from the restaurant at the top is fantastic. See it in the late evening when sky, water and buildings are stained lavender and rose by the sunset, and Istanbul takes on its most photogenic aspect of nostalgic mystery. West and south you look out over the Horn; east lies the Bosphorus and the Tophane district, marked by Sinan's Kılıç Ali Paşa Camii and a 19th-century westernized structure, Nusretiye Camii. Between the two stands a light-hearted rococo confection often depicted in old drawings of Istanbul—the Tophane Fountain.

One of the oldest subways in the world, the *Tünel*, starts below the tower near the Galata Bridge and rumbles a short distance to the beginning of İstiklâl Caddesi, the main street of Beyoğlu. Palatial embassies spread along the road from the late 17th century onwards; trees fanned graceful gardens and a brilliant cosmopolitan crowd promenaded the most fashionable avenue in town.

The embassies remain, reduced to consulates since the transfer of the capital to Ankara in 1923. At Galatasaray Square where İstiklâl Caddesi changes direction, a supremely elegant gateway announces Galatasaray Lisesi, the Franco-Turkish *lycée* which was founded in the 19th century and provided education for many of the great names in modern Turkish history.

Maybe change pace by side-tracking down **Çiçek Pasajı** (Passage of Flowers), a narrow lane to the left past the Galatasaray intersection, favourite haunt of the town's rowdy Bohemia. Best (and worst!) at night, it's crowded with a rag-tail, raucous bunch of gypsies, fortune-tellers, down-at-heel poets and visitors, all meeting, drinking and swapping yarns in innumerable taverns. A word to the wise: plant your

valuables in a safe place before you go.

A different experience awaits visitors to the **Pera Palas Hotel** on Meşrutiyet Caddesi, established in 1892 for Orient Express passengers. Its splendour is a little faded now but that only adds to the charm of the vast, chandeliered public areas with antique braziers and samovars and thick Turkish carpets. The cage-elevator will carry you up to view Atatürk's room, kept as it was when he stayed here.

Today's İstiklâl Caddesi is a busy commercial thoroughfare lined with boutiques, roaring with traffic. Yet, just here and there, you'll come across a high-ceilinged ice-cream parlour, a dignified pastry shop, redolent of the past.

The street ends at **Taksim Meydanı**, heart of the modern city, site of the big, new Atatürk Cultural Centre. In the summer, during the International Festival, concert tickets are sold here, and numerous performances staged.

Above Taksim is the "hotel district", and beyond again is the **Military Museum** (*Askeri Müze*), opposite the Sports

Palatial architecture, Anatolian folklore: Istanbul has both.

and Exhibition Hall at Harbiye. Don't be put off by its name: it's a fascinating place, and your visit will be all the more rewarding if you turn up in time for a concert by the Mehter Band, a revival of the Janissaries' music ensemble. Their brief, rousing displays are enjoyed by everyone, not least of all by the musicians themselves. (Performances are held every day at 3 p.m. except Monday and Tuesday.)

Dolmabahçe Palace

A broad road running downhill from Harbiye joins Dolmabahçe Caddesi, the tree-lined boulevard edging along the Bosphorus past Dolmabahçe Palace.

Pass through the ornately decorated gateway. There, dreaming among pines and magnolias, frosty white against the blue of the Bosphorus, is a 19th-century fantasy of scrolled and colonnaded marble, almost naive in its romanticism. In its way Dolmabahçe is symbolic. Built between 1843 and 1856 for Sultan Abdul Mecit, it was the residence of the last sultans. This dazzling exterior and a glittering interior provided the intimate setting for the final hours of the Ottoman Empire. Forced to admit the strength of Turkey's claims for democra-

cy, the last sultan left Dolmabahçe in a British warship.

When Atatürk opened the palace to the public he proclaimed that the "Shadows of God" (the sultans) had been replaced by "real people, who are not shadows" and ended, "I am here as the guest of the nation." The burst of applause was enough to set Dolmabahçe's chandeliers chiming like crystal bells.

For this is a crystal palace: there are 36 chandeliers hung throughout, complemented by numerous Baccarat and Bohemian fixtures, light fittings and mirrors; even the staircase leading from the entry-hall has a crystal handrail. Damask-covered chairs, alabaster bathroom, Sèvres vases, enamelwork, Gobelin and Turkish silk carpets, porphyry, porcelain, silver, two huge bearskins (gifts from the Tsar of Russia)—just to enumerate a few of the contents emphasizes the unreality of the last days of the empire.

Through this outdated world the spirit of Atatürk swept like a breeze. Early work on the westernization of the Turkish alphabet was carried out here. Atatürk maintained a small apartment for himself and died at Dolmabahçe on November 10, 1938. Palace clocks have been stopped at 9.05, the time of his death. (The palace is closed to the public Mondays and Thursdays.)

The **Maritime Museum** (*Deniz Müzesi*) and the **Painting and Sculpture Museum** (*Resim ve Heykel Müzesi*) are both in this area. Visit the latter for its landscapes showing Istanbul as a city of gardens and wooded hills, and to trace 19th- and 20th-century evolution of Turkish art.

Wooded hills are for real in **Yıldız Park**, as well as lakes, rivulets and winding paths. Two kiosks and a pavilion have been restored by Çelik Gülersoy, the man responsible for preserving many buildings from Istanbul's past. The palace here, **Yıldız Sarayı**, was a royal residence for 30 years in the time of Sultan Abdul Hamid II (1876–1909), who preferred it to Dolmabahçe.

Further up where the Bosphorus is narrowest broods **Rumeli Hisarı**, a fortress built by Mehmet II in 1452 in preparation for the Conquest and restored in 1953. Consisting of three major citadels linked by stone walls, it is a stupendous feat of construction, accomplished in only four months. Nowadays the interior contains a park and a theatre where folk-dancing and plays are performed.

Asian Shore

Ferries leave regularly from the northern end of the Galata Bridge for Üsküdar on the Asian shore. By car or coach you'll cross the Bosphorus higher up by the impressive Bosphorus Bridge, with a main span of 1,074 metres (3,524 ft.). This first bridge link between Europe and Asia was completed in 1973 for the 50th anniversary of the founding of the Turkish Republic.

At the Asian exit is **Beylerbeyi Palace,** less magnificent than Dolmabahçe but still a marvel of opulent furnishing and shimmering crystal, surrounded by gardens. It was reconstructed in 1865 on the site of an earlier palace, destroyed by fire.

The road which follows the Bosphorus northward leads to **Anadolu Hisarı,** a fortress facing Rumeli Hisarı on the opposite bank, which was built by the Turks as a preliminary to seizing Constantinople.

Directly inland from the Bosphorus Bridge, the park and lookout point of **Çamlıca** offers a bucolic refuge for viewing Istanbul. The extensive cypress-studded cemetery you see is **Karacaahmet,** one of the largest Islamic burial grounds in the world. South lies Üsküdar, better known to Europeans as **Scutari,** from where the ferries ply to the European shore. There, among many religious buildings, note **Iskele Camii** (1548), another mosque designed by Sinan for Suleiman's daughter, Mihrimah, and the **New Mosque of the Sultan Mother** *(Yeni Valide Camii),* dating from the early 18th century.

Scutari is associated with the name of Florence Nightingale. In bulky **Selimiye Kışlası,** the barracks sternly surveying the straits, the Lady with the Lamp set up her hospital for soldiers wounded in the Crimean War. Nearby is the well-kept Crimean War Cemetery.

Boat Excursions

No matter how many monuments you've visited or how much atmosphere you've absorbed, you still don't really know Istanbul until you've seen it from the water. All the main ferries leave from alongside the Eminönü end of the Galata Bridge.

Bosphorus

You'll weave from Europe to Asia and back again along the historic waterway, idling below pine-clad hills until you're within sight of the Black Sea. **59**

Some of the buildings will be familiar but from here they have a fresh aspect and you'll realize how carefully architects of long ago planned them with exactly this intention.

Outstanding among landmarks is **Kılıç Ali Paşa Camii** at Tophane, followed by the monumental 19th-century cannon factory. Then, looking like a stone ship about to push off into the water, comes the **Molla Çelebi Camii**, erected in the middle years of the 16th century. **Dolmabahçe Palace** sails into sight, almost shouldering the remains of **Çırağan Palace**, destroyed by fire in 1910, leaving only skeletal walls standing.

You'll chug under the leaping arch of the **Bosphorus Bridge**, to see **Beylerbeyi Palace** in Asia, the two vastly differing structures providing an illuminating juxtaposition of the introverted final years of the Ottoman Empire and the forward-looking aims of the Turkish Republic.

Next comes the most picturesque section, which may well tempt you to stop off for some leisurely exploring. On the Asian shore at Küçüksu and Anadolu Hisarı, calm streams, which Europeans called the Sweet Waters of Asia, emerge under dusky foliage. Mirrored beyond are some of the few re-

maining *yalı,* wooden houses built at the very lip of the water. Such summer dwellings, with a boat-house underneath, were designed for the enjoyment of two things most dear to the Turks: the sight of trees and flowers and the soft music of the water. Being costly to maintain, many were demol-

ished. But the last few have been renovated to make beautiful secondary residences for Istanbul's rich businessmen.

Rumeli Hisarı on the European side and **Anadolu Hisarı** opposite crouch in centuries-old defiance where the straits narrow. There—reconciling the two—is the startling-

Now a pleasant enclave of trees and lawns, Rumeli Hisarı is one of twin Turkish fortresses built prior to the Conquest.

ly modern 1988 Fâtih Sultan Mehmet Bridge. The apparent anachronism is best seen from Rumeli Hisarı's Sarahan Paşa Tower.

Afterwards comes the **Tarabya** district with its famous fish and seafood restaurants and cosmopolitan atmosphere. From Beykoz, the next stop in Asia, you can take a taxi to the Black Sea resort of **Şile** for excellent bathing beaches; Sarıyer in Europe is where you drop off for an equivalent excursion to **Kilyos**. Finally, there's Rumeli Kavağı (Europe) and Anadolu Kavağı (Asia), both sleepy villages whose fish restaurants make ideal luncheon spots.

Golden Horn

This is not a scenic trip in the normal sense but a view through the city's industrial back door at factories and shipbuilding yards all the way to **Eyüp**.

There, follow the crowds to the **mosque** *(Eyüp Sultan Camii),* supposed burial place of Eyüp Ensari, the Prophet Muhammad's standard-bearer. He came with an Arab army to besiege Constantinople and was killed by an arrow some time between 674 and 678. The grave was rediscovered as the result

Muslim rites hold an important place in Turkish family life.

of a vision; Mehmet the Conqueror built a shrine on the spot. He then had a mosque erected in 1458, his first in Istanbul and one of the most sacred in the Muslim world. It was visited by each sultan on accession to the throne for the ceremony of girding on the dynastic sword. In 1800 Selim III rebuilt the mosque.

There are many tombs in the environs, but the crowds are most intent on paying homage to Eyüp himself, interred in a tiled sanctum protected by a golden grid.

Behind the mosque is a tremendous hillside cemetery with many old turbaned tombs; a path winds up to a café known as the "Pierre Loti café", in honour of the French writer who often climbed to this windy summit, during his visit in 1876, to muse over the distant minarets of Istanbul melting into the twilight. One of Loti's relatives donated photographs from the period, now on display in an intimate museum.

Princes' Islands

When you need a rest from strenuous sightseeing, escape to this delightful retreat in the Sea of Marmara. Of the nine islands, **Principio** (Büyükada) is the largest and most visited. Runners-up are **Kınalı, Burgaz** and **Heybeli**. There are no museums, no cars even, just horses and carriages to get around (the alternative is riding a donkey), grand houses wreathed with wisteria and bougainvillea, pine forests, cliffs and swimming places.

You'll need a complete day for a leisurely visit, but avoid weekends when the whole of Istanbul has the same idea.

Bursa

The boat which goes to Princes' Islands usually continues to the little port and spa town of Yalova, from where land transport is available to Bursa. Coach tours and flights from Istanbul are available, too. The distance is far enough to necessitate an overnight stay.

The fringe of the Sea of Marmara is largely industrial. It has a ghostly look, especially in the early morning. Land, water and sky seem to merge, while steamers and rowboats pass like shadows, trailing dark lines in the colourless water as they cross towards Yalova.

Inland, the countryside takes on the gentle contours typical of this region, known in ancient times as Bithynia. Poplars and walnut trees flourish in the valleys, olive groves clothe the slopes; south of Gemlik the peach orchards begin. Then **63** there's a wide plain with Ulu Dağ, the Great Mountain, dominating the horizon, protective backdrop to Bursa.

This friendly, airy little city, founded in the 2nd century B.C. by King Prusias I, was known as Prusa after him. It became the Ottoman capital in the 14th century, then Edirne took over as seat of government in the 15th.

Outstanding among monuments is the **Tomb of Osman Gazi** *(Osman Gazi Türbesi),* founder of the Line of Osman and hence of the Ottoman Empire. He died in 1324 in the neighbouring town of Söğüt, but was buried in Bursa at his own request in what was formerly a Byzantine chapel. Lead plates in the dome once shone like silver. Complemented by the silver-embroidered drape on the sarcophagus, they caused his resting-place to be known as the "silver tomb". **Orhan Türbesi,** the tomb of Osman's son who lies nearby, was built on the site of a monastery. Fragments of its ancient mosaic pavement can be seen on the floor of the tomb.

The admirable **Green Mosque** *(Yeşil Cami)* takes its name from the dizzying beauty of its tiled interior. Both it and the **Green Tomb** *(Yeşil Türbe)* opposite were built by the same architect, Hacı Ivaz Paşa, for the 15th-century sultan, Mehmet I.

Stone from Bursa's own Great Mountain was quarried for the **Great Mosque** *(Ulu Cami),* constructed in the last years of the 14th century. Twenty domes crown its rectangular area; the central one, over the ablutions fountain, was originally left open, then glassed in later.

Take time, too, for the **Muradiye mosque complex,** built in the 1420s for Murat II, father of Mehmet the Conqueror, and the last sultan to rule from Bursa.

The town boasts a number of old-style houses with overhanging balconies shaded by vines. Call in to the 18th-century two-storey building, opposite the Muradiye, to see how wealthier private dwellings were furnished.

Bursa's other attractions include a newly reconstructed covered market, part of which extends into the **Koza Hanı,** first built in 1451. Nowadays this arcaded caravanserai is the centre of the silk cocoon market: look down from the rooms into the courtyard to see the cocoons being sorted and sold.

The Green Tomb in Bursa, once capital of the Ottoman Empire.

The most remarkable of all the thermal baths in the area is an Art-Deco marvel in the **Çelik Palas Hotel**. Right alongside, a 19th-century building garnished with wood-carving in typical Victorian colonial style houses the **Atatürk Museum**.

Two other museums merit a visit. Pigeons fly through the arched doorways of the **Museum of Turkish and Islamic Art** *(Türk ve İslam Eserleri Müzesi)* in the Green Mosque's *medrese*, one of the religious buildings which formed part of the mosque complex. The **Archeological Museum** *(Arkeoloji Müzesi)* in the Culture Park houses a number of Archaic, Hellenistic, Roman and Byzantine finds. (Both museums are closed Mondays.)

In the park, too, you may catch a display of Karagöz puppets. Although this type of shadow play probably originated in China, the characters which gained fame and affection in Turkey are based on two Bursa workmen, Karagöz and Hacivat. These were fellow labourers whose squabbles, jokes and tricks incurred the royal wrath of Sultan Orhan. They were put to death on his orders, but their earthy humour lives on, especially in Bursa where there is a modest monument commemorating them.

Aegean Coast

Unmatched for sun-drenched relaxation or for exploring a plethora of ancient sites, Turkey's Aegean coast is endowed with natural beauty. Izmir is a prime point for excursions to the ancient marble ruins. Most holiday-makers, though, choose to take their ease at one of the beach resorts further south—Kuşadası, Bodrum or Marmaris—and set out from there.

Northern Aegean

Because of its situation on the far north of the Aegean coastline, Troy can be reached equally well from Izmir, Bursa or Istanbul. Çanakkale is the main centre for the region. From there local travel agencies arrange tours to the sites.

Many visitors make a pilgrimage to the war graves in Gallipoli. This arm of land lying alongside the Anatolian coast presses the Sea of Marmara into the narrow strait of the Dardanelles (the Hellespont of antique times) before it joins the Aegean. Passenger-vehicle ferries make regular crossings. Tourist offices in Çanakkale and Gelibolu (Gallipoli) provide a map with each cemetery marked.

Gallipoli

Turkey entered World War I on the side of Germany and Austria. Allied operations in the Dardanelles aimed at securing an ice-free passage to Russia to supply arms and open another front. An abortive army-navy assault on Gallipoli, involving French and British forces, was launched in April 1915. On both sides thousands of men lost their lives. In November a freak blizzard accounted for hundreds more deaths, precipitating Allied withdrawal. Australia and New Zealand suffered tremendous losses. The Australian and New Zealand Army Corps (ANZAC) has given its name to Anzac Cove where some of the fiercest fighting occurred.

The whole peninsula is a vast memorial. Each cemetery is signposted; all are perfectly maintained, planted with flowers, scented by hedges of rosemary.

Troy

Seaside hotels south of Çanakkale, at Güzelyalı, provide an ideal spot for staying the night on the way to the ruins of the fabulous city which was, almost without doubt, Homer's Troy.

A small park at **Hisarlık** marks the entrance, and you can't miss the big wooden horse set up there. Beyond is everything—and nothing: those who come expecting grandeur will see just a limited area of excavations. For many, though, even with slight knowledge of the *Iliad* and the *Odyssey*, it's a magical place.

Here, according to legend most likely based on fact, lived peace-loving King Priam whose son, Paris, was inveigled by a trio of jealous goddesses into abducting the most beautiful woman in the world, Helen, wife of Menelaus, king of Sparta. The war which resulted between Greece and Troy lasted for ten long years. In it great heroes like Hector and Achilles met their death. The end came when the Greeks tricked the Trojans into dragging a wooden horse filled with armed men within their walls. They sacked the city and left it a ruin.

In fact, there were nine Troys over the centuries, from a primitive Early Bronze Age settlement existing from 3000 to 2500 B.C. (Troy I), to the Hellenistic and Roman metropolis which stood here from 334 B.C. to A.D. 400, known as *Ilium Novum*. Oblivion may have begun when Istanbul took commercial precedence over this trade centre for the Dardanelles.

Troy's location was relegated to the realm of scholarly debate until a German amateur archaeologist with a passion for Homer —Heinrich Schliemann—began excavations in 1871. Disorderly as his work was, at a time when archaeology was in its infancy, it was Schliemann's faith, personal fortune and boundless energy which uncovered Troy.

American archaeologists tend to identify Troy VIIa as Priam's city and place its destruction at about 1,260 B.C.; some eminent Turkish archaeologists disagree, attributing it to the level known as Troy VI. The second theory is certainly more appealing, for Troy VIIa was a mediocre, hastily constructed city, whereas its predecessor was a fine, solid town with a paved main street. It would be pleasant to think that the big southern gate was the Scaean Gate and that the large house supported internally by pillars was the palace of Priam. North-east are the remains of a well-built tower. Certainly, Troy VI fits more aptly with Homer's description of a "well-walled, well-towered, high-gated" city. It was razed by fire and earthquake. Yet Troy VIIa shows all the signs of a town under siege, with large subterranean food storage areas and confined accommo-

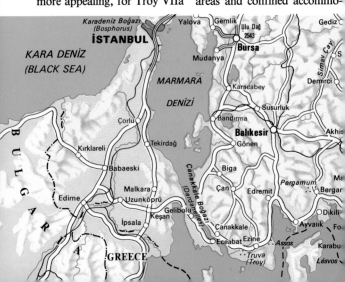

dation for numbers of people. Moreover, it was destroyed by war and swept by fire.

For detailed information it's best to hire a guide, although the site is signposted. The most casual visitor will sense drama in the timeworn stones. The wind whistles through thickets of stunted oak and sets the wild flowers nodding.

Schliemann's house is maintained as a small museum, with photographs of him and his wife. His memory still evokes enthusiasm and criticism. And, yes, he did find "Priam's treasure", a great haul of jewellery alongside the city walls of Troy II. He cut it out with a knife, wrapped it in his wife's shawl and smuggled it away. It was last seen in Berlin but vanished during World War II.

On the coast, glorious beaches fringe the Gulf of Edremit, with Mount Ida to the east and, west, the lovely outline of the Greek island of Lesbos. Ayvalık is an ideal spot for enjoying it all. South again, Dikili is a picturesque fishing port.

Pergamum

Perched above the modern town of Bergama, Pergamum (or Pergamon) was, at its height, ruled by the Attalids, put into power by Alexander

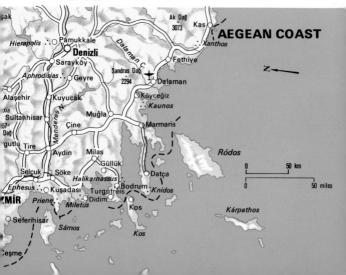

the Great's general, Lysimachus.

Three basic areas attract visitors: the Asclepion, the centre of town and the acropolis.

Above the entrance of the **Asclepion**, one of the most reputed medical centres of the ancient world, was written: "Here death is forbidden by order of the gods". Dedicated to Asclepius, god of healing, rivalling similar centres at Epidauros, Kos and Ephesus, the Asclepion provided hot baths, massage, cures by drinking water from a spring latterly found to be mildly radioactive, and primitive psychiatry. Rational treatment, plus a good measure of faith, reached a peak when Galen (130–200), the "prince of physicians", practised here.

Entry is along a monumental road bordered by columns. A library, theatre and public toilets were provided. The open-roofed "cure centre" was threaded with channels to provide the therapeutic sound of running water for patients; afterwards their dreams were analyzed for diagnosis.

The remains of the city of the

Pergamum was famed for its fine buildings and medical cures.

Attalids rise on a series of artificial terraces. See the ruins of the **Pergamene library**, near the temple of Athena, goddess of learning. The Attalids loved books and managed by fair means and foul to build up a collection of some 200,000 manuscripts. When Alexandria's library was destroyed by fire, Antony gave Cleopatra all Pergamum's books.

The biggest building on the acropolis is the **Trajaneum**, erected in the 2nd century for the deified Roman emperors, Trajan and Hadrian.

Set in the hillside, the **theatre** is a tighter half-moon shape than most, and impressively steep. East Berlin's Pergamum Museum was the recipient of a remarkable frieze—one of the finest existing examples of Hellenistic sculpture, representing the Battle of the Gods and the Giants—which enhanced the nearby Altar of Zeus, built to commemorate the defeat of the Gauls in 190 B.C. Other temples, gymnasia, fountains, agoras, palaces and houses all attest to the artistic and economic achievements of Pergamum.

Many examples of votive offerings to Asclepius are in the **Bergama Museum,** along with other finds from the area and Turkish-Islamic objects.

Izmir and Environs

This sparkling city, still often known by its Greek name of Smyrna, is well served by air, land and sea. In the summer there's a regular overnight ferry from Istanbul (heavily booked) with cabin accommodation. If you're driving from the north, detour to the superb beach villages of Yeni Foça and Eski Foça. The latter is the site of ancient Phocaea, whose mariners were described by Herodotus as "the pioneer navigators of the Greeks". They founded dozens of colonies, one of which, Massilia, became Marseilles. By road or sea you'll be treated to a memorable view of Turkey's third largest metropolis, spread around the shores of a beautiful bay.

An Aeolian colony established themselves north of the bay in the 10th century B.C., afterwards replaced by Ionians, also from the Greek mainland. The poet Homer, who was probably born in Smyrna, belonged to this brilliant civilization. Later, Alexander the Great visited and refounded the city around Mount Pagus as the result of a dream he had there. When the Ottoman Turks arrived, they allowed Europeans to install trading stations, and Izmir grew wealthy handling 71 merchandise from the interior, including Smyrna figs and Turkish tobacco. It prospered as a Levantine port until almost completely destroyed by fire in 1922, at the close of the Greek-Turkish war. Rebuilt on the former site, just where Alexander wanted it, today's city of 800,000 people is as animated as ever, but almost no trace remains of its past.

From the port a broad boulevard, Atatürk Caddesi, popularly called the Kordon, stretches through the heart of town. Horses decked with blue and orange pompoms draw spanking *faytons* for a sightseeing tour, taking in the south-east headquarters of NATO, Cumhuriyet Meydanı (Republic Square) with its equestrian statue of Atatürk, and finishing at Konak Square. The tiny mosque, Konak Camii, was built in 1756; nearby is the city's symbol, a curlicued clock-tower dating from 1901. Local ferries stop here, and it's also the starting-point for municipal buses.

Take the overhead bridge to the **bazaar,** less exciting than Istanbul's but jam-packed with goods, the whole paraphernalia of daily living. It's a great deal more wide-awake than the Roman marketplace or Agora, built in the 2nd century, now an idyllic retreat of bleached grass where lizards bask in the sun. There are remains of a colonnade. Statues of gods are grouped in reduced circumstances in the north-west corner, but the best finds have been removed to the **Archaeological Museum** *(Arkeoloji Müzesi)* in the Culture Park.

Kadifekale ("the Velvet Castle"), Izmir's flat-topped guardian, is Mount Pagus of antiquity. The view is exceptionally fine over the Agora and Konak Square to the bay, where ferries ply across blue water to the opposite shore.

Sardis

Sardis, one-time capital of Lydia, used to be the wealthiest city in the world. Logically enough, the Lydians invented coined money, most of it stamped with a lion's head, the royal emblem of the city. Under Croesus, the last king (560–546 B.C.), coins of pure gold and silver were minted. The gold was washed down by the River Pactolus; the Greek historian Herodotus relates that specks of the precious metal were caught in the fleece of sheepskins spread in the shallows, giving rise to the legend of the Golden Fleece. Sardis was overrun by the Persians, terminating the reign of

Croesus and the Lydian monarchy. Later the city regained importance, only to be destroyed by Tamerlane in 1401.

The village of Sart stands near the ruins. Most imposing is the **Temple of Artemis**, an enormous structure boasting some of the finest Ionic capitals ever excavated. A 5th-century Byzantine church leans up against it. Above, a fairly tough climb away, is the Acropolis.

Across the highway from the temple, a majestic 3rd-century synagogue has been restored with American funds, as have remains of shops outside the walls. These were apparently part of a complex which included the gymnasium, the whole a handsome example of Roman architecture.

Manisa

Nearby Manisa, formerly Magnesia ad Sipylum, was capital of the Byzantine Empire for a brief period in the 13th century, when the emperor withdrew here to escape from the Crusaders. Originating from Magnesia in Northern Greece, early inhabitants claimed to be the first Greeks in Asia. Classical ruins are almost non-existent but there are several fine Ottoman religious buildings, one of which has been converted into a museum.

Spring and summer deck the slopes of Mount Sipylus with myriad wild flowers—violets, cyclamen in thousands, hyacinths and the Sipylus tulip, with pointed flame-coloured petals, which provided the original bulbs for this favourite flower of Ottoman times and subsequently for the Dutch tulip industry. At the foot of the mountain there's a bas-relief of Cybele, the Anatolian mother-goddess.

Other Sites

Colophon, Notium and Claros are accessible by road via the town of Değirmendere, south of Izmir. Colophonians were extremely wealthy in their time; they dressed in purple robes and smothered themselves in perfume to frequent the marketplace. This extravagance, combined with gourmandizing habits, attracted the criticism of early historians and brought about the city's downfall. In time Colophon merged with Notium, which became known as New Colophon. The ruins are scanty in both places. Claros was not a city but the site of a temple and oracle of Apollo, whose proximity provided the source of Colophon's wealth. The temple has been excavated but is practically covered by river water.

Teos is not a major destination, but it's such a thoroughly delightful spot that it's worth a visit. Turn off at Seferihisar for the village of Siğaçik and drive through orange groves towards the island-studded bay. You'll feel as though you've found *your* archaeological site. Here there are no ticket offices, no souvenirs and almost certainly no other visitors. Appropriate gestures in the local grocery will unearth a friendly villager quite prepared to meander with you through the ruins. The old Agora is a melon field; sky-blue convolvulus twines among blocks of the bluish Teian marble-like limestone quarried still near Seferihisar. For full enjoyment, bring a picnic. The road continues to the sea.

Çeşme

The forked peninsula thrusting west from Izmir has a real jewel in the little town of Çeşme.

The pristine whitewash on the houses is all the more startling when the *imbat*, an invigorating sea breeze, blows, setting coloured carpets flapping against shop balconies. But the **beaches** are the main attraction. Golden Dolphin Holiday Village has one of Turkey's rare casinos and there are many other hotels around the Bay of Boyalik with, for good measure, a thermal pool in the sea at Ilica. There's motel, bungalow and *pansiyon* accommodation too, often offering thermal facilities, for the water is reputedly good for respiratory and rheumatic complaints.

There are few monuments—which may well come as a relief. Çeşme does have its 14th-century Genoese fort, a small one, and a rather grand caravanserai alongside. Some 14 miles (22 km.) away, Ildır is the site of the ancient city of Erythrae, but even there the beautiful situation takes precedence over the ruins.

Central Coastal Area

Some of the privileged storks of this world have their nests on old stone columns along the Izmir–Selçuk road which leads on to **Kuşadası**. The name, meaning "Island of Birds", refers to a small promontory. Apart from a small fort on Güvercin Adası and a 17th-century caravanserai converted into an hotel, ruins are thin on the ground in the Kuşadası area itself, dedicated to the good life of boating and bronzing. There could be no more pleasant spot for doing just those things, blessed as it is with crystalline water, golden sand and fish that almost pop out of the sea onto the plate. But when

thoughts do turn to exploring further than the next palm tree, there's plenty of history nearby and some left over.

One of the best-preserved and most-visited of all the Aegean cities, Ephesus, lies 17 kilometres (10½ m.) inland. Many other remains dot the countryside, for this region is

The windmill turns, the world changes; tradition endures.

Ionia, famous in ancient times for the softness of its landscape, the kindness of its climate, the lushness of its valleys. It vies with Greece itself for numbers of monuments.

Ephesus

Ephesus was among the greatest of ancient cities. Founded before the 10th century B.C. by Ionian Greeks (who gave this area of coast its old name), it was ruled in turn by Croesus, king of Lydia, Cyrus, king of Persia and the Attalids, kings of Pergamum. The last Attalid bequeathed Ephesus to Rome. At its height there were 200,000 inhabitants. Camel caravans brought the exotic treasures of the East; Greece, to the west, supplied suitable gods for worship. Queen of them all was Artemis (Diana), whose personality of virgin huntress merged with the role of an Anatolian

fertility goddess, Cybele. The great Temple of Artemis, one of the Seven Wonders of the World, was erected in her honour. Intellectually, spiritually and commercially, this was one of the most splendid cities ever known. But the greatness of Ephesus was linked to its port. When the harbour silted up in the 3rd century, the city went into a decline. The site was rediscovered in 1869 by a British engineer-archaeologist after six years' searching. Most of what

Homemaker or hopeful fisherman, you'll enjoy the Aegean coast.

St. Paul's friends begged him not to confront angry crowds in the huge theatre at Ephesus.

you see belongs to the Roman imperial period.

Tours usually begin at the Magnesian Gate. The well-preserved **odeum** is here, and next to it the **Prytaneum,** or Town Hall, where the two statues of Artemis in the Ephesus museum were found. Walk down the marble street called Curetes Way. The Temple of Domitian and the marvellously restored **Temple of Hadrian** were dedicated to the emperors-cum-gods. The adjoining Baths of Scolastica were a large complex including a brothel, with its entrance at the south corner of Marble Street. Keep an eye out for the signs carved into a paving-stone indicating the way.

The **Library of Celsus,** a miracle of restoration, was built

are the **Twin Churches of Mary**. The original Roman basilica was used as a commercial building, then transformed into a church on whose ruins two later churches were raised.

A charming legend is attached to the **Cave of the Seven Sleepers**, between Ephesus and Selçuk at the foot of Mount Pion, telling of persecuted Christian lads who slept here for two centuries, then awoke to find Christianity the state religion.

The small town of **Selçuk**, not far from Ephesus, has several noteworthy monuments. The 6th-century **Basilica of Saint John** marks the spot where the Apostle spent his last years and died. Down the hill is **Isa Bey Mosque** (1375). The daunting fortress atop the hill dates from Byzantine times. Don't miss the museum, even if it's only to see the two statues of Artemis.

in the 2nd century by a Roman consul as memorial and tomb for his father. Air channels ran behind the niches storing the manuscripts, to control humidity.

The **Great Theatre**, set with its back to Mount Pion, could seat 25,000 people. Drama and music fans still crowd into the theatre each spring during a local festival.

The **Arcadian Way** advances grandly from the theatre to the port. Behind the **Gymnasium**

The **Virgin Mary's House** *(Meryemana)* lies outside the city on what used to be known as Mount Coressos (now Bülbüldağı). Here Mary is thought to have spent her last days. The house's foundations seem to be 1st century, and the location was discovered some 100 years ago through the visions of a German nun, Anna Katharina Emmerich. It's long been a place of pilgrimage. **79**

Inland to Pamukkale

You can take a day trip to Pamukkale from Kuşadası or Izmir, but it's tiring. Try instead to stay overnight and enjoy the thermal pools, also to visit Aphrodisias, not the most publicized but one of the best of all the ancient sites.

The road runs through the rich valley of the river the Greeks knew as the Maeander.

Turn off past Kuyucak for **Aphrodisias,** 38 kilometres (23 m.) away. In the distance hovers Baba Dağı, "Father's Mountain", with snow folded in the ridges even in midsummer. The Aphrodisias site is at the village of Geyre and the museum is well worth a visit for cult statues of Aphrodite, discreetly gowned, looking particularly well-behaved for a goddess of love.

Not much remains of her temple, but the **stadium** is enormous, possibly the finest in the ancient world, with a length of 228 metres (748 ft.) and seating capacity for 30,000, still put to use at festival time.

The recently excavated theatre is outclassed for charm by a small **odeon** with a semicircular

80 *Below Hieropolis lie the pools and pillars of Cotton Castle.*

pool. It's the sort of place you feel Aphrodite would have chosen herself: dragonflies hover above waterlilies, doves coo in the bushes and petals from wild pomegranate trees drop in scarlet showers onto white marble.

The main highway proceeds past a turnoff to Laodicea. Hold your breath from here on because across the plain, pillared by stalactites, shining like an alabaster palace, towers Pamukkale, the **Cotton Castle**. Hot thermal springs pouring from Çal Dağı have created this limestone formation of scalloped basins and cascading water, looking for all the world as though carved out of ice and cloud by some angelic hand.

Above it stood Hieropolis, the "Holy City", named for its quantity of temples; nowadays they are replaced by hotels, where you can swim in natural warm pools. For a unique experience visit the Turizm Hotel enclosing the **Sacred Pool,** the realm of watery deities. Buoyant water floats you above fluted marble and broken Corinthian capitals. Cedars and oleanders shade the source of the spring.

The remains of Hieropolis include the Roman baths, the theatre and a big necropolis which is thought to contain the tomb of the Apostle Philip. Before returning to the coast visit Ak Han, a 13th-century Seljuk caravanserai.

Other Sites

The Ionian coast between Kuşadası and Bodrum has a cluster of three major sites which can be seen in one day.

Priene, once one of the most active ports in the Ionian Confederation, now stands several miles inland as a result of the silting up of the Maeander River. In spite of Roman alterations it's basically an ancient Greek city, particularly interesting for its grid layout.

The big **Temple of Athena** retains several of its Ionic columns. It was still being built when Alexander the Great arrived in 334 B.C., and he paid for its completion. The theatre, a temple to Zeus and the Bouleterion ("Council House") are other main buildings; a fairly short climb brings you to the Sanctuary of Demeter and Kore (Persephone), the oldest of the holy places in Priene.

Miletus today is set above melancholy marshes where frogs croak at nightfall, seeming to mourn the downfall of this erstwhile stronghold of maritime power, one of the principal ports and centres of the Greek world. In the 8th and 7th centuries B.C. Miletus established almost 100 colonies. The landscape has completely changed over the years; many of the ruins are subjected to regular flooding, but the Graeco-Roman theatre is superb.

Didyma has only one monument, a Temple to Apollo. No city ever stood here, just this colossal temple, one of the largest and most elegant of ancient times, renowned for its oracle. When the Persians under Darius destroyed Miletus in 494 B.C. they destroyed Didyma's temple, too. For several centuries it was under reconstruction but was never completed—you'll see that some of the columns have been left unfluted.

Bodrum

Bodrum is set against an unbelievably blue sea. The flat-roofed, square-built houses are almost blinding under the hot sun, their white walls festooned with great clusters of purple bougainvillea. Luxurious yachts crowd the marina, an international crowd enlivens the streets and keeps the night young with music and dancing. It's all easy-going, fun-loving, with a touch of cosmopolitan Bohemia, the St. Tropez of Turkey.

Bodrum's old name is Halicarnassus, capital of the former region of Caria. Herodotus, the "Father of History", was born here. Mausolus was the most famous ruler; his mausoleum (the word comes from his name) was one of the Seven Wonders of the World.

Apart from remains of the theatre and sections of the city wall, the only surviving ancient monument is the **mausoleum,** and there's not much left of that. The area where it stood is an open-air museum. Mausolus started building it himself around 355 B.C. Destroyed by earthquake, it was quarried by the Knights of St. John to help build the 15th-century **Castle of St. Peter** which still dominates today's port and city.

Now an amazing museum, the stupendous fortress was constructed when the Knights were forced out of Smyrna by Tamerlane.

The castle towers represent the various tongues under which the knights were grouped: hence there is an English, French, German and Italian Tower, plus the Serpentine Tower.

There's a tremendous view from the top of the towers, and you'll be able to look down into the boatyards of Bodrum, where many a prestige yacht is still built according to the centuries-old traditions of the region.

Bodrum is not the spot for swimming but there is no lack

Ride the ship of the desert in sight of the ships of the sea.

of paradisiacal beaches in the area. Boat tours make a day trip, leaving Bodrum at 9-10 a.m., visiting beaches all the way to Karaincir, and returning at about 6 p.m.

The ancient site of **Knidos** across the bay on the Marmaris peninsula can be visited by boat on a day trip. With more time and at more expense, you can arrange a trip in the Gulf of Gökova, between Bodrum and Marmaris. It really is a boatman's dream—uninhabited islands, fish aplenty, forested shorelines and sandy beaches.

Kos lies off the coast of Bodrum; there's a regular ferry service to this Greek island.

Marmaris

Translucent waters and a shoreline edged with dark conifers and contrasting pink oleanders give this town a peaceful, pic-

turesque air. Amusing carriages pulled by miniature tractors take you off to the nearby beaches; boats ferry passengers around the bay to more dramatically beautiful spots, for this is one of the most indented areas of the whole coast. The Greek island of Rhodes is a 3 hour trip away by ferry. The town is served by Dalaman Airport, some 100 kilometres (62 m.) away.

There's little to remind you that Marmaris is ancient Phys-cus, belonging to the Carian kingdom. The fort is 16th-century. No ruins, but pleasant little Turkish houses, shops still managing to stock an astonishing quantity of antiques—from stilted bath-clogs to brass coffee-grinders—and enough restaurants and discos to keep you happily occupied when the sun goes down. A great place for families, with the added advantage that you can swim from early June to the last days of September.

And it's here that the Aegean meets the Mediterranean, with the long, pine-laden peninsula as dividing-line. To its west is the fishing village of Datça.

South-east of Marmaris, **Fethiye**, ancient Telmessus, overlooks an island-strewn bay. You can't miss the many Lycian sarcophagi and rock-hewn tombs behind the town, of which the most imposing is the 4th-century B.C. tomb of King Amyntas. It's like a small palace, fronted by two Ionic pillars.

Stop off along the way at Köyceğiz to visit another fishing village, Dalyan, and the ruins of the Carian city of Caunus. The theatre is well preserved, along with a handful of buildings, and below the acropolis are numerous rock-cut tombs peculiar to this part of the world. Ölü Deniz lagoon offers idyllic bathing.

The site of **Xanthus**, not far from Kinik, boasts especially famous Lycian tombs once decorated with sculptured reliefs, now replaced by plaster casts.

Viewed from both Fethiye and Xanthus, the sea is an intense turquoise, unlike the paler hues further north. It's a sign that you've already left the Aegean and are now looking out over the waters of Turkey's Mediterranean coast.

What To Do

Shopping

Bazaars, markets and shops all over Turkey are full of exciting things to buy. Many of the goods make their way to Istanbul but some are better —and cheaper—in their own areas. Fixed prices are becoming more common but when you do bargain, bargain with firmness. You'll make friends, not lose them. And if you're offered tea or coffee during the process, accept it as a perfectly sincere gesture.

Carpets, of course, are at the top of the list. A quick distinction here: carpets are knotted, kilims are woven and have no pile. Both originated as floor and wall coverings for nomad dwellings; no two are alike. You can learn to "read" the symbols which convey such ideas as true love, protection against the Evil Eye or desire for a child. Age, rarity and (when applicable) the number of knots per square centimetre influence the price. Experts rely largely on touch to assess the quality of wool and silk and test

Master craftsmen take pride in individual workmanship.

whether dyes are chemical or natural.

Rarity apart, the most expensive are silk. A cheaper version exists, mixing silk and artificial fibres. These can make attractive wall hangings but won't stand up to use on the floor. You will see few really antique carpets and if you do come across one it will have to be cleared for export. The merchant should take care of the formalities. Many dealers are genuinely helpful, and should point out which are machine-made articles. The more you talk with them, the more likely you are to recognize real worth.

Turkish towels are renowned worldwide. They were invented in Bursa for a sybaritic sultan who wanted instant drying power when he left the bath. He organized a competition to find it. A Bursa man won, and Bursa still manufactures the best towels.

Handbeaten objects in **copper** and **brass** gleam from dozens of shops and workshops. Bakırcılar Caddesi in Istanbul's Beyazıt district is a good street to go looking. Turkish braziers are marvellously decorative and come in many shapes and sizes. Or what about launching out on a shoe-shine box like the ones put to good use in the streets? Less weighty is the huge selection of lamps, candlesticks, coffee-grinders, long-handled pots for making Turkish coffee, and samovars. Turkish artisans will also take pride in crafting copper and brass objects to your own requirements.

Crystal is appealing and cheap, **ceramic plates** make a pleasant souvenir and so do Turkish **tiles.** The best are old ones from Iznik, but in Bursa you'll be presented with a wide choice of new tiles in traditional blues and greens. **Onyx** turns up everywhere: the factory near Pergamum can create individual articles. **Meerschaum,** a white, claylike mineral, is carved into pipes and figurines. Or you could stun friends back home with a *nargile* (water pipe).

As for **jewellery,** the best finds are in the bazaars. Main fashion streets also have jewellery boutiques. Gold is normally sold by weight, with something added for workmanship. The current gold price is displayed by the shop; if in doubt you can check in the daily paper.

Some of the **textiles** are exquisite and so is the **embroidery.** Look for blouses in raw cotton *(şile bezi)* or headscarves *(yemeni)* edged with handmade lace *(oya)*. Socks and stockings knitted in Central Anatolia carry bright designs. Small needlework purses represent hours of work.

Leather and **suede goods** offer bargains for men and women, and the quality of the skins is superb. You can have shoes custom-made by small craftsmen; more typical is the bejewelled Turkish slipper.

All sorts of **spices,** including henna and snuff, are for sale in Istanbul's Spice Market, where you can also unearth herbal pick-me-ups.

Flying carpets have landed! Scene on a Kuşadası rooftop.

You will run across a fair number of **antiques** including coins, glassware, samovars and Ottoman pieces. A small flea market springs up near the Istanbul Book Market every Sunday. Some shops specialize in taking elements of antique Turkish jewellery and working them into attractive necklaces, bracelets and earrings. Usually silver, they're often enhanced with niello. Of course, you have to keep an eye out for reproductions, and if you're offered a "Byzantine icon", take it with a pinch of salt.

And, to appeal to a variety of tastes and budgets, there are fake swords and daggers, *karagöz* marionettes traditionally cut from camel parchment, blue beads to protect you against the Evil Eye or Muslim prayer-beads *(tespih)* in every imaginable material, including plastic, olive-wood and agate. Or maybe you could learn to play the *saz,* the musical instrument resembling a mandolin. Pamukkale produces an intriguing souvenir: statuettes are soaked in mineral water until they become coated with lime. At Kuşadası, Bodrum and Marmaris you'll see sponges in all shapes and sizes, while Bodrum's hand-crafted leather sandals are chic, cool and practical.

Entertainment

Belly-dancing is typically oriental, and every Turkish girl can do it. As performed by the best dancers, scantily clad in shimmering gauze, it's subtle, graceful and erotic. There are certain basic figures, but generally the girls invent as they go along, pivoting the lower part of the body, scooping up their long hair, using a horizontal head movement and accompanying it all with constant arm and hand gestures to the sound of small cymbals. The top performers are at the top nightspots, hence the most expensive.

Floorshows with a tourist slant will also include folk dances which vary according to their regions of origin. You may see the *Horon*, a Black Sea dance where men clad in black and silver quiver like fishes caught in a net to the music of a primitive violin, or maybe the Sword and Shield dance of Bursa, depicting the Ottoman conquest of the city, enacted to the clash of weapons. Clacking wooden spoons provide the

Easy to learn and bound to cause a sensation back home!

rhythm for the lively Spoon dance (Kaşik Oyunu).

Turkish-style supper clubs (gazino) provide Turkish dancing, music and a programme of assorted performers; a taverna is similar, usually with a more exuberant atmosphere. Discos and nightclubs are much like their Western counterparts. Turks seize any occasion for dancing, usually to a cocktail of Western and Turkish music, although they're at their most uninhibited with the latter. Trying is the best way to learn the national style of dance, but it helps to have a Turkish partner to imitate.

Turkish music falls into several categories: folk songs, classical compositions, largely from the 18th century, and the popular westernized type you hear on the radio. The annual Istanbul Festival (mid-June to mid-July) gives summer visitors the occasion to enjoy a variety of artistic offerings. Tickets are sold at the Atatürk Cultural Centre, Taksim Square. Don't miss rousing displays by the Military Band, presented most days at the Military Museum. The brilliantly garbed performers play kettledrums, clarinets, cymbals and bells with a gusto that sets your ears ringing.

The Istanbul State Opera reaches a high standard in a repertoire of Western and Turkish works, performed from October to May at the Atatürk Centre. There, too, during the same period, are regular concerts by the Istanbul State Symphony Orchestra, recitals by Turkish and foreign artists and performances by the State Ballet.

Turks excel at backgammon (tavla), and almost any coffee-house produces a formidable crop of players. However, coffee-houses are considered a "men only" preserve. That effectively precludes women from having a go at water pipe smoking. Lots of coffee-houses have pipes for hire and will prepare one.

There are seven casinos in the country, where you'll find most of the usual games.

Don't leave without trying a Turkish bath, preferably in one of the famous baths like Cağaloğlu Hamamı in Yerebatan Caddesi, an 18th-century beauty well used to foreigners, or the even older (16th-century) Galatasaray Hamamı. The experience is sensuous, cleansing and relaxing, but the architecture alone makes a visit worthwhile. Note there are usually separate entrances for men (erkek) and women (kadın), but sometimes special hours or days are designated. You undress in a cubicle, then, enveloped in a towel, proceed via a steamy side-room to the centre slab in the hot room, where you are rubbed down by the attendant with a special bath mitt to remove impurities from the skin. If the treatment is too enthusiastic you have only to indicate, and, should the heat become oppressive, you can escape into a cooler room. Thus steamed, honed, massaged and probably a few pounds lighter, you emerge feeling on top of the world.

Well, who wouldn't want to show off in a setting like this!

Sports

Water Sports

Swimming. Istanbul's main hotels have swimming pools for guests. Non-guests can take out seasonal membership for the facilities at the Etap Marmara and the Hilton.

The best beaches within reach of the city are the attractive Black Sea resorts of Şile and Kilyos. In summer a bus leaves Üsküdar for Şile every half hour from 7.30 a.m. to 6 p.m. For Kilyos, on the European side, catch the Bosphorus boat from Eminönü, disembark at Sarıyer, then hire a taxi ·or *dolmuş.*

Cosmopolitan resorts, fun and friendship: Turkey, today.

There's swimming on the Princes' Islands, too, but avoid the weekends and the crowds. The Bosphorus is not recommended for cleanliness; nor are the nearer beaches on the Sea of Marmara. Florya is a popular resort there, but slippery bright-green seaweed in the shallows may put you off. Further along the northern Marmara, past Silivri, are far nicer white sand beaches, especially around Gümüşyaka and Sultanköy.

The Aegean coast offers innumerable opportunities for superb bathing. The choice is infinite, from popular holiday resorts to forgotten coves and thermal pools.

Boating. Whether you hire a craft or you're here under your own steam, the Aegean coast is the ideal place for boating enthusiasts. Hired vessels come with or without crew,

along the Aegean and Mediterranean coasts.

The best boating season is May to October. In the summer months the *meltem* or etesian wind blows from north-west to south-east on the Aegean, and can create choppy seas in the afternoon. It lasts about 40 days. Around Izmir and Kuşadası they call it the *imbat*.

Official sources advise that it's best to avoid zig-zagging between Turkish and Greek waters. Archaeological finds should be left where they are: if discovered on board, the boat can be confiscated.

Fishing. Line and net fishing is permitted without a licence in any non-prohibited area (if in doubt, check with the local tourist office). Fishermen can always be found to take you out with them for a day's sport.

but make your arrangements early—there aren't enough to go round. The celebrated Blue Voyage *(Mavi Yolculuk)* offers unrivalled opportunities for swimming, picnicking and sightseeing on shore. It's a yacht cruise organized by various agents, lasts a week and can be taken out of Kuşadası, Bodrum, Datça, Marmaris, or Fethiye and Kas on the Mediterranean. Don't forget other cruise possibilities: maybe a full two weeks out of Istanbul Spear-fishing and scuba-diving are allowed only if you are accompanied by an official Turkish guide.

Other Activities

Skiing. Uludağ near Bursa is the "in" place for winter sports, with chair-lifts, ski-tows, slalom and giant slalom courses, beginners' slopes, instruction and a fashionable après-ski scene. The season is January to April.

Larger Aegean resorts of- **95**

fer **wind-surfing** and **tennis**. In Istanbul, non-members are accepted at the Tacspor tennis club, Yenigelin Sokak. 2, Suadiye (coaching available).

Spectator Sports

The country's national speciality is **oil wrestling** *(yağlı güreş)*. Kırkpınar near Edirne is the place to see it. Competitions are held in June, when muscular participants in leather pants, coated all over with oil, perform a ceremonial march before flinging each other around, to the cheers of thousands. Or, even more extraordinary, catch up with a bout of **camel wrestling** *(deve güreşi)* at Selçuk, near Kuşadası. Camels are far from sweet-tempered at the best of times. In this sport two moody males express mutual antagonism by sparring together until one is established as the victor, and the other is dragged off to get over the insult. It's exciting, and the animals are not exposed to serious injury.

After all that excitement, **horse-racing**, held at the Veliefendi Hippodrome near Bakırköy, some 15 kilometres (9 m.) from Istanbul) might seem rather tame. Meetings take place from April to December, then horses and punters move to

Eating Out

Gastronomes rank Turkish cuisine as one of the best in the world—third after French and Chinese. It's inexpensive by most standards, and customers are invariably treated with courtesy in even the smallest restaurant. If the menu poses problems, it is quite acceptable to enter the kitchen and point out what you want to eat.

The setting is often as memorable as the meal, especially if you dine outdoors along the shores of the Bosphorus or the Aegean. A starry sky, a whisper of oriental music, vines shadowing old stone walls, the lapping of water nearby and, if you're lucky, a moon big enough to look as though it's hired for the occasion.

Starters

Meze is the name given to an enormous selection of appetizers, both hot and cold. They can represent a meal in themselves, so until you feel in the swing of things, avoid ordering a main dish until you've sampled them.

Cold *meze* are usually presented on a tray at your table for selection. Try stuffed mussels, Turkish pastrami cured with red pepper, chopped cu-

cumber and yoghurt pepped up with garlic, smoked oxtongue, mashed fava beans.

Dolma means stuffed vegetables, usually peppers, aubergines, tomatoes or vine leaves. Good Turkish bread or *pide* (unleavened bread) adds to your enjoyment of a variety of dips: maybe fish roe mixed with lemon juice and oil *(tarama),* grilled aubergine whipped with lemon or yoghurt *(patlıcan salatası)* or thyme-flavoured

Whether your taste is takeaways or dainties fit for a pasha...

yoghurt *(haydariye).* Traditionally, *rakı* is drunk with them all.

Perhaps you'd prefer hot entrées like spiced mutton liver *(arnavut ciğeri),* wafer-thin pastries stuffed with cheese or minced meat *(muska böreği)* or fried mussels *(midye tava).*

Soups

What about soup: "wedding soup" *(düğün çorbası),* lamb broth flavoured with lemon, thickened with beaten egg; red lentil soup *(kırmızı mercimek çorbası);* or mutton tripe soup *(işkembe çorbası)?* Turks swear by this one as a remedy for a hangover.

Fish

When they tell you the fish is fresh, they mean it. You can run the gamut from swordfish *(kılıç),* bluefish *(lüfer),* tunny *(palamut),* mackerel *(uskumru)* and red mullet *(barbunya)* to sardines and anchovies. In Istanbul the smart fish restaurants are at Tarabya on the Bosphorus, but they're good anywhere in the city and along the Aegean coast. Seafood, likewise delicious, is expensive.

Main Courses

Kebabs (skewered, grilled meat) are a speciality: famous *şiş kebap* is lamb and tomatoes served with rice. Lamb and beef roasted on a vertical skewer, then thinly sliced, is called *döner kebap.* There are various meat and vegetable stews, easier to identify on the spot in the kitchen than by their names on the menu.

Vegetarians will be in their element—there are so many meatless dishes that you don't need to look for a special restaurant. Rice pilaf *(pilav)* is satisfying, cracked wheat pilaf *(bulgur pilavı)* even more so.

Desserts

You'll think you're back in the harem when you come to the desserts. "Lips of the beloved" *(dilber dudağı)* and "lady's navel" *(hanım gobeği)* are both fried delicacies. Nightingale's Nest *(bülbül yuvası),* walnut-stuffed pastry, is shaped like its namesake; familiar *baklava* is a pastry with walnuts or pistachio nuts. All are served with syrup.

Highly recommended are the milk puddings and various sweetmeats. Turkish Delight *(lokum)* is the best-known, but there's also *helva* which represents a whole category of sweets in Turkey. And, of course, delicious fruit: ripe peaches, plump nectarines, yellow melons from Çeşme, strawberries, pears, cherries and grapes.

The hazelnuts and almonds are excellent. Turks like their almonds served unroasted and chilled. You'll see pedlars wheeling their wares past restaurants at night, with the almonds laid out on a block of ice and a flaming gas lamp to light the way.

Beverages

Rakı, an aniseed liqueur, can be drunk throughout the meal either neat or with water, whereupon it assumes a pearly colour. Half-and-half is a

Sophistication or simplicity. The choice is there.

reasonable mixture for beginners; advanced students could test themselves on beer and *rakı,* popular with Turkish soldiers. Beer consumption is high, the quality good. Locally produced vodka, cognac, whisky and gin are an honourable and less expensive substitute for imported brands.

Turkish wines *(şarap)* have a tradition going back to 7000 B.C.; European vine-stocks may well originally have come from here. Nevertheless, despite the quality products available, Turks are not great wine drinkers, and only a small proportion of the harvest goes into wine-making and from there onto the home market. Still, there's a full range of reds, rosés, whites and sparkling wines; the standard is high, sometimes exceptional. The same is true of liqueurs with a fruit, coffee or cocoa base. Sour cherry *(vişne)* is especially delectable.

Of course, you may well settle for bottled water, in which case remember that here "mineral" water *(maden suyu)* means the fizzy variety. Beverage specialities are refreshing *ayran,* yoghurt whipped with water, and *boza,* a calorie-packed sourish drink made from fermented millet, at its **100** best in pudding shops where it's served sprinkled with cinnamon.

Coffee *(kahve)* means Turkish coffee, strong and well-brewed, poured grounds and all into tiny cups without milk or cream. Specify the degree of sweetness you want when you order: *sade* (without sugar), *az şekerli* (slightly sweetened), *orta şekerli* (sweet), or *çok şekerli* (very sweet). Leave it a minute to let the grounds settle.

Tea *(çay)* is grown near the Black Sea and, served throughout the day in waisted glasses, it's the cup of friendship, drunk hot and strong without milk.

Snacks

Sample a round sesame-seed roll *(simit),* sold from little stalls and trays wherever you go. Corn on the cob is another kerbside treat. Pizza bars are springing up everywhere; the real Turkish-style pizza is the *Karadeniz pidesi* originating in the Black Sea area. On the Aegean coast you'll find that cucumbers *(salatalık)* are a great thirst-quencher. Barrow salesmen peel them, you salt and pepper to taste. Or bite into a slice of watermelon *(karpuz).* Ice-creams, sherbets and cakes are all highly recommended. Naturally, buy only from stalls where the hygiene seems up to standard.

What's Cooking?

It helps to know your restaurants in Turkey, for there are several varieties, some of them specializing in specific dishes. When you start responding to those wafting odours, here's a list to make things easy.

Lokanta	Serve Turkish food, but may offer a set menu or a "tourist menu" including non-Turkish dishes.
Ahçı dükkanı, Aşçı, Aşevi	A more modest version of the above with no pretence to anything but local dishes, therefore usually cheaper and more authentic.
Kebapçı	Experts in grilled meat, especially kebabs served with *pide* (unleavened bread) and rice. Beverages are soft drinks and *ayran* (drinking yoghurt) but you can send out for beer.
Pide salonu, Pideci	Turkish pizza parlour. Flat bread served hot with meat or cheese and fresh green salad. A good, inexpensive luncheon stop.
Köfteci	Specialists in *köfte*, a minced lamb croquette, frequently garnished with a string-bean salad.
Büfe	Recognizably related to a buffet anywhere. Sandwiches, hamburgers, sometimes *döner kebap*, toast, cool drinks including yoghurt, no hot drinks.
İşkembeci	Tripe-soup vendors whose wares are a traditional pick-me-up for the *rakı* before. Some add calf's foot, brains and tongue to their highly recommended remedies.
Birahane	Beer-houses where you can buy or send out for accompanying titbits like mussels and shrimps. Wine and *rakı* also available.
Pastahane	A rather grander version of a *tatlıcı*: pastry and candy shops.
Muhallebici	Boiled chicken, chicken soup and pilaf are served, as well as local pastries and delicious milk-based desserts including custards and rice pudding. Inexpensive, and to heck with the calories.

BLUEPRINT for a Perfect Trip

How to Get There

Because of the complexity and variability of the many fares, you should consult an informed travel agent well before your trip.

BY AIR

Scheduled Flights

The major international airport in western Turkey is Istanbul's Atatürk Hava Limanı (see also p.107), with services from Europe, the Middle East and the U.S.A. There are, however, also direct international flights into Izmir. Most flights from South Africa go via a European city, while those from Australia and New Zealand mainly connect by way of London.

Charter Flights and Package Tours

From the U.K. and Ireland. Many operators offer traditional air-and-hotel packages to Istanbul (and to Izmir on a smaller scale). There is a reasonable number of flight-only operators to Turkey.

From North America. Istanbul is not featured in charter flights and only rarely in package tours; however it does appear on cruises taking in Greece and the Greek Islands.

From South Africa. Turkey is mainly featured on cruises in conjunction with Greece. Ask your travel agent.

From Australia and New Zealand. Tours of Turkey are available from certain operators, taking in Istanbul, Çanakkale, Izmir and Bursa (including cruising the Bosphorus). Istanbul also appears on some Eastern European and Balkan tours.

BY SEA

During the season, there are regular car-ferry services to Istanbul from Venice and to Izmir from Venice and Ancona. Ferries also ply between some of the Greek islands and ports on the Aegean coast.

BY RAIL

Direct daily trains run from Munich to Istanbul, with sleeping cars as far as Belgrade. The journey is long (1½ days), uncomfortable, smoky, crowded, but cheap. Another train leaves Venice in the late afternoon and arrives in Belgrade the next morning. You then have a long wait for the afternoon train to Istanbul, 26 hours away.

BY CAR

Motorists going from Europe to Istanbul can choose either the roads of Bulgaria or those of Greece. If you prefer the first alternative, you need a transit visa; for the second solution, more time. The road through Bulgaria takes you via Belgrade, Niš and Sofia to Edirne and Istanbul; the one through Greece, via Belgrade, Niš, Salonica and Ipsala or Edirne. (For driving regulations in Turkey, see pp. 113–115.)

You can considerably reduce driving time either by loading yourself and your car onto an auto-train for part of the journey or by taking a car ferry from Italy (see above).

BY BUS

Several companies operate regular bus tours from cities in Europe (Athens, Hamburg, Munich, Paris, Vienna, etc.) to Istanbul. From Munich, an express bus makes the journey in about 40 hours.

When to Go

The best periods to visit Istanbul and the Aegean coast are spring and autumn, April–May–June and September–October–November. The Marmara and Aegean regions have a typical Mediterranean climate, with hot summers and mild winters. The hottest and driest period is July–August; the coldest is January–February, the rainy season, with 72–83% humidity in Istanbul.

		J	F	M	A	M	J	J	A	S	O	N	D
Average daily max.	°F	46	47	51	60	69	77	82	82	76	68	59	51
in **Istanbul:**	°C	8	9	11	16	21	25	28	28	24	20	15	11
and in **Izmir:**	°F	55	57	63	70	79	87	92	92	85	76	67	58
	°C	13	14	17	21	26	31	33	33	29	24	19	14
Average daily min.	°F	37	36	38	45	53	60	65	66	61	55	48	41
in **Istanbul:**	°C	3	2	3	7	12	16	18	19	16	13	9	5
and in **Izmir:**	°F	39	40	43	49	56	63	69	69	62	55	49	42
	°C	4	4	6	9	13	17	21	21	17	13	9	6

Planning Your Budget

To give you an idea of what to expect, here are some average prices in Turkish liras (TL). However, take into account that all prices must be regarded as *approximate,* and that the inflation rate is high.

Airport transfers. Taxi to Istanbul centre about 13,000 TL, shuttle bus 1,000 TL.

Buses. Standard fare in Istanbul 350 TL, Blue Card 20,000 TL.

Car hire (international company, high season, July–September). *Renault 12* 44,000 TL per day, 440 TL per km., 750,000 TL per week with unlimited mileage. *Ford Sierra* 82,000 TL per day, 802 TL per km., 1,450,000 TL per week with unlimited mileage. Add 10% tax.

Cigarettes. Turkish brands 600 TL per packet of 20, imported brands 2,200 TL.

Hairdressers. *Woman's* cut 5,000 TL, shampoo and set or blow-dry 8,000 TL, permanent wave 50,000 TL. *Man's* cut 5,000 TL, shave 3,000 TL.

Hotels (double room with bath and breakfast). Luxury class $179, 1st class $125, 2nd class $75, 3rd class $37.50, 4th class $35.

Museum entry. 10,000 TL.

Restaurants. Hotel breakfast 10,000 TL, lunch/dinner in fairly good establishment (table d'hôte) 20,000 TL, bottle of wine 10,000 TL, Turkish coffee 2,000 TL, small bottle of beer from 2,000 TL, soft drink (small bottle) from 1,500 TL.

Shoe shine. 1,000 TL.

Shopping bag. Bread (½ kg.) 500 TL, butter (250 g.) 2,500 TL, cheese (½ kg.) 6,000 TL, potatoes (1 kg.) 600 TL, beefsteak (1 kg.) 8,500 TL, coffee (100 g.) 2,200 TL, milk (1 l.) 1,300 TL, soft drink (1 l.) 1,250 TL, bottle of wine 5,000 TL.

Turkish bath. 15,000 TL.

Underground/Subway (Istanbul). 500 TL.

An A–Z Summary of Practical Information and Facts

> Listed after many basic entries in the appropriate Turkish translation, usually in the singular, plus a number of phrases that should help you when seeking assistance.
>
> For all prices, refer to the list on p. 105.

A

ACCOMMODATION (See also CAMPING). The Turkish Ministry of Culture and Tourism has rated some of the hotels, motels and boarding houses from luxury to fourth class. Those with top rating offer the maximum comfort on a par with international standards. Many other establishments, especially on the Aegean Coast, are checked by municipal authorities.

Registration at your place of residence involves completing a form with a few simple questions, usually translated into English, and presenting your passport. Check whether breakfast, VAT (12%) and service charge (15%) are included in the room rate.

Hotels *(otel)*. Most big towns have either first- or second-class hotels. Luxury establishments are virtually confined to Ankara, Istanbul and Izmir. In every case, refer to the *Hotel Guide* published by the Ministry of Culture and Tourism, available at all tourist information offices.

Flats/Apartments *(apartman dairesi)* and **villas** *(villa)*, furnished and unfurnished, may be hired in Istanbul—a cheaper alternative than a hotel room for long stays. Watch for the sign "Kiralık" ("For Hire") or contact a real estate agent (broker).

Motels *(motel)* fall into three categories. They're nearly always equipped with shower, toilet and a radio; some include air-conditioning and a fridge. Normally they sleep two people, but managements are generally cooperative about putting in extra beds for children, or you can hire two units side-by-side and open them into a suite for families.

Holiday villages *(tatil köyü)* in seaside areas, classed A and B, provide furnished flats—sometimes, but not always, with cooking facilities. They all have a shop and restaurant near at hand, and most have a swimming pool.

Boarding houses *(pansiyon)* on the Aegean Coast offer a more
intimate glimpse of Turkish life. The larger are licensed by the Ministry. Those under the control of the municipality are simpler. Breakfast is included in the price and there may be a kitchen where you can cook and share a fridge. Toilets and bathroom are usually communal. Single and double rooms and some units with cooking facilities are also available. But cheapest of all is a dormitory where you share the room with up to five others.

Youth hostels *(talebe yurdu)* offer benefits to holders of International Student Travel Conference (ISTC) or International Youth Hostel Federation (IYHF) cards and visitors with "student" or "teacher" on their passport. (Note that ISTC cards also allow reductions on Turkish domestic and international flights, domestic and international maritime lines, trains, and on entrance to museums, cinemas and concerts.) Youth hostels are generally open between July and September.

AIRPORTS *(havaalanı)*

Istanbul. All incoming and outgoing internationl and domestic flights for Istanbul are at Atatürk Hava Limanı, 24 km. (15 miles) out of town. Here you'll find all the usual facilities: banks, information office, baggage deposit, duty-free shops, boutiques, restaurants and cafés, car hire, trolleys, etc. Porters wear grey uniforms with identification badges. They're generally reliable, but may try to overcharge if you pay in foreign currency.

Turkish Airlines (THY, *Türk Hava Yolları*), the national airline, run a bus service about every 15 minutes from the airport to Şişhane Air Terminal in central Istanbul (30 minutes) with return every 30 minutes.

Izmir. The international airport of Adnan Menderes, 15 km. (9 miles) from the city, has similar facilities. Buses run to the city centre, and trains leave regularly for Basmane railway station.

Note that minimum check-in time is 1 hour on domestic routes, 2 hours for international departures.

Domestic flights. Around 15 cities in Turkey are linked by frequent domestic flights, making air travel a recommended means for travelling long distances. The Istanbul-Bursa flight takes about 30 minutes; Istanbul-Izmir, 40 minutes; Istanbul–Dalaman, 1 hour 15 minutes. **107**

A   THY propose interesting reductions for families, sports groups, students (aged 12 to 26/28) and children on both domestic and international flights.

Porter, please!	**Hamal, lütfen!**
Take these bags to the bus/taxi, please.	**Lütfen bu çantaları otobüse/taksiye götürün.**

ANTIQUITIES *(antika eşya).* The purchase of antiquities is strictly prohibited, so assure yourself that the treasure you have acquired is not classified as an object of historical value, liable to be confiscated at customs and, potentially, land you in trouble. Be prepared to show a bill on departure. Old coins are particularly protected. The merchants from whom you buy should be able to advise on all the formalities.

C   **CAMPING** *(kamping).* Campsites registered with the Ministry of Culture and Tourism are limited in number but generally offer showers and toilets, kitchen and laundry facilities, a shop and electricity. They are open April/May to October. Especially recommendable are the sites operated by the Mocamp-Kervansaray, which are also licensed by the Ministry. You may camp outside organized sites provided you make yourself known to village authorities and, of course, request permission from the owner to set up on private land, but it is wiser to choose a place where there are other campers. Tourist information offices will help.

Is there a campsite nearby?	**Yakında kamping yeri var mı?**
Can we camp here?	**Burada kamp yapabilir miyiz?**

CAR HIRE *(araba kiralama).* (See also DRIVING.) International and local car-hire firms have offices in the major cities, as well as representatives at the international airports. Ask about reduced rates for weekly or monthly rentals, or any special seasonal deals. The main cars for hire are the *Fiat/Murat 124* and *131,* and *Renault 12,* which are all assembled in Turkey.

To hire a car, the driver must have a valid driving licence or an International Driving Permit. Depending on the company and the car, the minimum age is 19, 21, 25 or 28. A deposit is usually required unless you pay by credit card, accepted by the larger firms. Permission for a second person to drive the car should be requested from the rental agency when the car is taken out, otherwise the insurance is void.

Independent travellers should look into the "Fly-and-Drive" programmes offered by various travel agencies.

I'd like to hire a car (tomorrow)	**Bir araba kiralamak istiyorum (yarın).**
for one day/a week	**bir gün/bir hafta için**
Please include full insurance	**Lütfen, sigortası da tam olsun.**

CLOTHING. (See also WHEN TO GO, p. 104.) Istanbul is hot in the summer but can turn chilly or windy, so take a sweater or jacket. A certain formality is expected in cities. Turks have a strong sense of elegance and like to dress up, especially in the evening. A short gown, which is not too revealing, and dressy shoes for women, a lightweight jacket or suit and tie for men, will prove suitable evening wear. Casual, light clothes are the answer for the coast, but include something stylish for dining and dancing. Hats, sunglasses and flat shoes are a must for archaeological sites.

Modesty will win respect. Decolleté tops, miniskirts and shorts are unsuitable everywhere except on the beaches. Allowances are made for foreign visitors, but dress according to Turkish standards for entering mosques, where everyone should remove their shoes; bare arms should be covered (heads when praying). Sometimes scarves are provided, but it's a good idea to carry one on you.

COMMUNICATIONS

Post offices *(postane)* are identified by the letters PTT in black on a yellow background. Small offices are open Monday–Friday only till 5.30 p.m. and may close for lunch. Large hotels have post offices or will handle your mail for you at the desk. The main Istanbul office, Büyük Postahane at Sirkeci, near the European-side railway station, operates around the clock, weekends included, for buying stamps, sending mail, telegrams, telexes and for telephoning. It is advisable to send all foreign mail by air. Street mailboxes are painted yellow.

Poste restante (general delivery) letters should be sent care of the central post office *(Merkez Postanesi)* in the town of your choice.

A domestic express postal service *(acele posta servisi)* exists in Istanbul and Izmir, handling non-perishable goods and documents up to 2 kg. (4.4 lb.) in weight.

Telegrams *(telgraf)* can be sent normal, urgent *(acele)* or lightning *(yıldırım)* for Turkish destinations; normal or urgent for other countries.

C **Telephone** *(telefon)*. The telephone system is getting better all the time. Tokens for booth telephones are sold at post offices. Many shops allow customers to use the phone. Direct dialling is available to nearly all countries. If you go through the operator for long-distance communications, there's a choice of normal, urgent or lightning service. Only some countries can be called reverse-charge (collect). The direct-dialling codes to some main Turkish cities are:

Adana	711	Çanakkale	1961
Ankara	4	Istanbul	1
Bursa	24	Izmir	51

Have you received any mail for me?	**Bana posta var mı acaba?**
A stamp for this letter/postcard, please	**Bu mektup/kart için bir pul, lütfen.**
express (special delivery)	**ekspres**
airmail	**uçak ile**
registered	**taahütlü**
I want to send a telegram to ..	**... (ya) bir telgraf yollamak istiyorum.**
Can you get me this number in Ankara?	**Lütfen bana Ankara 'da şu numarayı, bağlayabilir misiniz?**
reverse-charge (collect) call	**ödemeli**
person-to-person (personal) call	**ihbarlı**

CONSULATES and EMBASSIES *(konsolosluk; elçilik)*. Embassies moved from Istanbul to Ankara when the capital was transferred. If problems develop, get in touch with your consulate or embassy:

Australia   Embassy: Nene Hatun Caddesi 83, Gaziosmanpaşa, Ankara; tel. (4) 136 12 40

Canada   Honorary Consul-General: Mr. Yavuz Kireç, Büyükdere Caddesi, Bengün Han 107, Kat 3 Kayrettepe, Istanbul; tel. (1) 172 51 74
Embassy: Nene Hatun Caddesi 75, Gaziosmanpaşa, Ankara; tel. (4) 136 12 75

Eire   Honorary Consul-General: Mr. Ferruh Verdi, Cumhuriyet Caddesi, Pegasus Evi 26a, Harbiye, Istanbul; tel. (1) 146 60 25. (The nearest embassy is in Rome.)

New Zealand   The nearest embassy/consulate is in Athens; U.K. consulate in Istanbul will advise if necessary.

South Africa	The nearest embassy/consulate is in Athens.
U.K.	Consulate: Meşrutiyet Caddesi 34, Tepebaşı, Beyoğlu, Istanbul; tel. (1) 144 75 40
	Embassy: Şehit Ersan Caddesi 46a, Çankaya, Ankara; tel. (4) 127 43 10
U.S.A.	Consulate: Meşrutiyet Caddesi 104–108, Tepebaşı, Beyoğlu, Istanbul; tel. (1) 151 36 02
	Embassy: Atatürk Bulvarı 110, Kavaklıdere, Ankara; tel. (4) 126 54 70

CONVERSION CHARTS. (For distance measures, see DRIVING.) Turkey uses the metric system.

Length

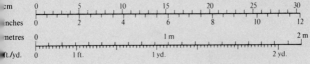

Weight

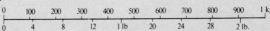

Fluid measures

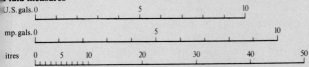

COURTESIES. (See also MEETING PEOPLE.) You don't need to be stiffly polite but old-world courtesy still prevails in this rather formal society, and circumspect behaviour wins friends. City dwellers are more relaxed than people in smaller places; try to understand and accept patterns of behaviour. For instance, women are not really welcome in coffee houses. Family values are upheld. Revealing clothing creates an unfortunate impression and can provoke antagonism. If something doesn't go your way, irritation and raised voices are less effective than quiet insistence.

C

From the poorest to the richest, Turks traditionally treat visitors a honoured guests. Hospitality is generous, spontaneous and sincere Offers of cigarettes, tea and coffee will probably occur several times a day; feel free to accept and respond in kind. When visiting a privat house, you may be invited to remove your shoes. Flowers or perfum are appropriate gifts for the hostess. Letters of thanks, a postcard o photographs are naturally appreciated.

In mosques, keep a respectful distance from people at prayer.

CRIME and THEFT. Aggression towards visitors is rare. However pickpockets (men *and* women) of considerable talent and originalit sometimes work in crowded places. One of their favourite ruses i starting a minor scuffle to attract your attention. Moral: deposi valuables in the hotel safe.

Narcotics offences, even minor involvement, are punishable by ex tremely severe prison sentences. Black-market moneychangers shoul be avoided.

CUSTOMS and ENTRY FORMALITIES. (See also DRIVING.) Mos visitors, including British and American, need only a valid passpor to enter Turkey; British subjects can even travel on the simplifiec Visitor's Passport. No vaccination certificates are required.

The following chart shows what main duty-free items you may tak into Turkey and, upon your return home, into your own country:

	Cigarettes	Cigars	Tobacco	Spirits	Wine
Turkey	400	or 50	or 200 g.	5 l.*	
Australia	200	or 250 g.	or 250 g.	1 l.	or 1 l.
Canada	200	and 50	and 900 g.	1.1 l.	or 1.1 l.
Eire	200	or 50	or 250 g.	1 l.	and 2 l.
N. Zealand	200	or 50	or 250 g.	1.1 l.	and 4.5 l.
S. Africa	400	and 50	and 250 g.	1 l.	and 2 l.
U.K	200	or 50	or 250 g.	1 l.	and 2 l.
U.S.A	200	and 100	and **	1 l.	or 1 l.

*in opened bottles, 3 l. of which may be whisky
**a reasonable quantity

Valuable items including jewellery, tape recorders, transistor radios and similar objects should be registered in your passport on entry to ensure they can be taken out again when you leave. The purchase and export of antiquities is prohibited.

Currency restrictions. Any amount of local or foreign currency may be imported. However, foreign currencies should be specified in the passport upon arrival in order to avoid difficulties on departure. Local currency up to the equivalent of U.S. $1,000, and foreign currencies up to the amount imported, may be taken out of the country.

Keep exchange slips since you may need to present them when reconverting Turkish money into foreign currency and when taking souvenirs out, as proof that the goods were purchased with legally converted currency.

I've nothing to declare. **Deklare edecek birşeyim yok.**

DRIVING. To bring your car into Turkey you'll need:

- a valid driving licence or an International Driving Permit (recommended)
- car registration papers
- a nationality plate or sticker
- international insurance certificate (Green Card) or alternatively third-party insurance. *Note:* make sure it covers both the European and Asian part of Turkey.

Since you'll probably be travelling through other countries on your way to Turkey, inform yourself about their national regulations, too, at your local automobile association and insurance company. For stays exceeding three months, you will need to apply to the Turkish Touring and Automobile Club (*Türkiye Turing ve Otomobil Kurumu,* TTOK) for a triptyque or *carnet de passage.*

At the Turkish border, the car must be registered in your passport. You have to carry *two* reflector warning triangles and a first-aid kit. Motor-cyclists and passengers must wear crash helmets. Drive on the right.

Speed limits are 50 k.p.h. (31 m.p.h.) in urban areas, 70 k.p.h. (43 m.p.h.) just outside some cities and 90 k.p.h. (56 m.p.h.) on the open road. Cars towing caravans (trailers) are restricted to 40 k.p.h. (25 m.p.h.) and 80 k.p.h. (50 m.p.h.) respectively.

Driving conditions. Drive on the right, overtake (pass) on the left. Most motorways (expressways) are toll free; there's a small toll for

D vehicles crossing from Europe to Asia on the Bosphorus bridge (it's free on the return). Most parts of the country can be reached by well-maintained highways; country roads are more adventurous.

Employ extra caution at all times: the accident rate is high. Normally the calmest of people, Turks lose all their inhibitions behind the wheel of a vehicle. Bus drivers are the worst offenders. Keep an eye out for bicycles, pedestrians, horse carriages and wandering livestock. Night driving should be avoided; many vehicles are not lit—and therefore invisible until you're upon them. If you injure someone, you're quite likely to be surrounded by hostile villagers.

Traffic police, accidents. In the event of an accident, the police must be informed immediately *whether anyone has been injured or not;* the law requires that a police report be filed. Traffic police are understanding with foreigners, but strict about offences. You can be fined on the spot. Radar control is used and police checks are frequent.

Note: Drinking and driving to any extent is strictly forbidden in Turkey. Insurance cover for a hire car involved in an accident may well depend on your taking an alcohol test at the time to confirm that you had not been drinking.

Breakdowns. Mechanics in Turkey are highly skilled and carry an unbelievable choice of spare parts due to the fact that they spend a lot of time patching up the older model cars you still see on the roads. However, since some foreign models may stump them, carry any spare parts you feel you may need. If you have the misfortune to break down, someone will almost certainly pull up to lend a hand or at least give you a lift to the nearest garage. You can also call the Turkish Touring and Automobile Club which will help you get repairmen.

For the **Istanbul** area, they are at Halaskargazi Caddesi 364, Şişli; tel. 13 14 63 1

For **Izmir:** Atatürk Bulvarı 370; tel. 21 71 49

If you are holder of a letter of credit, or traveller's protection cover, from your home automobile association (i.e. AA's 5-Star Service), the TTOK will make the necessary repairs and send the bill to your home country. The TTOK gives road assistance to members of the major motoring organizations, and pays the expenses of transporting a damaged vehicle to the motorist's home country.

Note: if it is necessary to leave a vehicle behind in Turkey, it must be brought to the nearest customs office or local administrative authority to have the registration of the vehicle cancelled in your passport; only **114** then will you be free to leave the country.

Distance **D**

Road signs. Most road signs are the standard pictographs used throughout Europe. However, you may encounter some written signs:

Azami park 1 saat	Parking allowed for 1 hour
Bozuk yol	Poor surface
Dikkat	Caution
Dur	Stop
Durmak yasaktır	No stopping
Klakson çalmak yasaktır	Sounding of horn forbidden
Hastane	Hospital
Kaygan yol	Slippery road
Park yapılmaz	No parking
Tamirat	Roadworks (Men working)
Yavaş	Slow down

(International) Driving Permit	**(uluslararası) ehliyet**
car registration papers	**araba ruhsatı**
Green Card	**yeşil kartım**
Can I park here?	**Buraya park edebilir miyim?**
Are we on the right road for...?	**... için doğru yolda mıyız?**
Full tank, please.	**Doldurun, lütfen.**
normal/super/diesel/unleaded	**normal/süper/motorin/ kursunsuz benzin**
Check the oil/tires/battery, please.	**Yağı/Havayı/Aküyü kontrol edebilir misiniz, lütfen.**
I've had a breakdown.	**Arabam arzalandı.**
There's been an accident.	**Bir kaza oldu.**

ELECTRIC CURRENT. You will find both 110- and 220-volt, 50 cycles A.C., so check before you plug in. **E**

What's the voltage—110 or 220?	**Voltaj kaçtır—yüz on veya iki yüz yirmi?**
I need an adaptor/a battery.	**Ek adaptör/pil istiyorum.**

EMERGENCIES. Your first recourse will be to find somebody who speaks English. Emergency telephone numbers are listed on the first page of the directory.

E Istanbul:

Police, tel. 166 66 66
Tourist Police, tel. 527 45 03

Depending on the type of emergency, refer to other entries in this section such as CONSULATES, HEALTH AND MEDICAL CARE, LOST PROPERTY, etc.

G **GUIDES and INTERPRETERS** *(rehber; çevirmen)*. Travel agents are obliged to employ guides on all tours. Otherwise, official guides wearing a black-and-white badge can be found at the entrance to major sites. They work for a set fee. You can also arrange to hire a guide from the local tourist office. To contact the Guides' Guild in Istanbul, tel. 140 25 23.

Interpreters can be found through the chamber of commerce:

Istanbul: Hal Yolu, Eminönü; tel. 526 62 15

Izmir: Atatürk Caddesi 126; tel. 13 41 19

Or you could enquire at your consulate.

We'd like an English-speaking guide.	**İngilizce bilen bir rehber istiyoruz.**
I need an English interpreter.	**İngilizce bilen bir çevirmene ihtiyacım var.**

H **HEALTH and MEDICAL CARE.** There are no vaccination requirements, but ask your doctor about any inoculations or tablets recommended for protection. To be completely at ease, take out adequate travel insurance to cover any risk of illness and accident while on holiday. Your travel agent or insurance company at home will be able to advise you.

Large hotels have doctors on call. Medical standards are high, but since there are long queues at public hospitals, it would be best to contact a private hospital in case of need. Istanbul has a long list of foreign hospitals, including the American Hospital:

Güzelbahçe Sok. 20, Nişantaşı; tel. 131 40 50

Many doctors (as well as dentists and pharmacists) speak a language other than Turkish.

To avoid stomach upsets, wash and peel all fruit and vegetables well, and don't be too ready to sample cooked food (except pretzels) from itinerant street vendors.

Take the sun in easy doses at first (only 15 minutes direct exposure for the first day or two), and avoid heat exhaustion (wear loose clothes and drink plenty of fluid).

Pharmacies, identified by the sign "Eczane", are open from 8 a.m. to 8 p.m. The address of an all-night pharmacy will be posted in the window. If it appears closed when you get there, ring the bell and wait. Pharmacies supply most medicaments, including antibiotics, without a prescription. Some drugs (even common ones, like certain types of headache tablets) are occasionally in short supply, so if you think you'll be in need of a specific product, bring it with you.

For cosmetics and perfume, you can also go to a *parfümeri* or a department store.

Where's the nearest pharmacy?	**En yakın eczane nerededir?**
Where can I find a doctor/ a dentist?	**Nereden bir doktor/bir dişci bulabilirim?**
an ambulance	**bir ambülans**
hospital	**hastane**
sunburn	**güneş yanığı**
sunstroke	**güneş çarptı**
a fever	**ateş**
an upset stomach	**mide bozulması**

HITCH-HIKING. Motorists are well-disposed to giving foreigners a ride, but with bus travel so cheap, it's really not worth the bother. Hitch-hiking is not recommended for women on their own.

LANGUAGE. Turkish is very distantly related to Finnish and Hungarian. It is written in the Roman alphabet, introduced as one of Atatürk's reforms in the 1920s, and is characterized by the use of suffixes to modify meanings, resulting sometimes in amazingly long words.

French used to be the main second language; now it's English, with German-speakers on the increase. Tourist officials and staff in larger hotels speak English. Even people who don't will make a real effort to understand.

L The pronunciation of some Turkish letters:

c like **j** in **j**am
ç like **ch** in **ch**ip
ğ almost silent; lengthens the preceding vowel
h always clearly pronounced
ı like **i** in s**i**r
j like **s** in plea**s**ure
ö approx. like **ur** in f**ur** (like German *ö*)
ş like **sh** in **sh**ell
ü approx. like **ew** in f**ew** (like German *ü*)

If you want to try Turkish, consult the Berlitz phrase book *Turkish for Travellers*. It covers practically all the situations you're likely to encounter during your Turkish travels.

Following are a few phrases you'll want to use often:

Hello	**Merhaba**	Good night	**İyi geceler**
Good morning	**Günaydın**	Good-bye	**Allahais-**
Good afternoon	**İyi günler**		**marladık*/**
Good evening	**İyi akşamlar**		**güle güle****

Do you speak English?   **İngilizce biliyor musunuz?**
I don't speak Turkish.   **Türkçe bilmiyorum.**

LOST PROPERTY. Because of language problems, it's wisest to ask the Tourist Police to contact other offices for you. Property lost on Istanbul buses can be claimed from İETT Taşıtlar Daire Başkanlığı, Büyükdere Caddesi, Şişli.

Turks who find a child in distress will act with kindness and concern.

I've lost my wallet/handbag/   **Cüzdanımı/El çantamı/**
passport.   **Pasaportumu kaybettim.**

M **MAPS.** The Ministry of Culture and Tourism provides free maps through tourist offices. The maps in this book were prepared by Falk-Verlag, Hamburg who also publish a map of Istanbul.

I'd like a street plan of...   **...şehir planını istiyorum.**
a road map of this region   **bu bölgenin yol haritası**

* if you're leaving
** if you're staying

MEETING PEOPLE. You'll probably have to speak first to strike up a conversation, but once you do you'll feel people are delighted you've broken the ice. Friendship is sincere and enduring.

Turkish girls are under strict parental control; transgression of traditional Turkish standards of morality could land foreign gentlemen in tricky situations. Turkish men, although fascinated by Western "freedom" in relations between the sexes, usually think in terms of marriage, home and family.

| How do you do?/How are you? | **Nasılsınız?** |
| Very well, thank you. | **Çok iyiyim, teşekkür ederim.** |

MONEY MATTERS

Currency. The monetary unit is the Turkish pound, *lira* (abbr. TL).
Coins: 5, 10, 20, 25, 50, 100 TL.
Banknotes: 100, 500, 1,000, 5,000 and 10,000 TL.
For currency restrictions, see CUSTOMS AND ENTRY FORMALITIES.

Banks *(banka)* are open from 9 a.m. to 5 p.m., Monday to Friday, with a lunch break from noon to 1 or 1.30 p.m. After hours, money can be exchanged at major hotels. At Istanbul's airport and Sirkeci railway station, currency exchange offices *(kambiyo)* stay open without breaks to accommodate passengers. Exchange of foreign currency at banks and hotels is quick and trouble-free. Remember to take your passport for identification, and keep the exchange slips.

Eurocheques, traveller's cheques, credit cards *("eurocheque"; "traveller's cheque"; kredi kartı)*. Eurocheques can be changed at central offices and larger branches of major banks like Türkiye İş Bankası. Major credit cards are accepted by hotels and establishments used to dealing with visitors. Traveller's cheques can be changed at major banks like Türkiye İş Bankası and large hotels. The latter may charge commission. Always present your passport for identification. For dining out in smaller places, you're better off relying on cash, and when bargaining, you'll find a merchant more prepared to drop his price for a cash sale.

I want to change some pounds/ dollars.	**Sterlin/Dolar bozdurmak istiyorum.**
Do you accept traveller's cheques?	**Seyahat çeki kabul eder misiniz?**
Can I pay with this credit card?	**Bu kredi kartımla ödeyebilir miyim?**

M **MUSEUMS AND MONUMENTS.** Many of Istanbul's museums and monuments are closed one or two days a week. The following will help you plan your sightseeing hours.

Archaeological Museum *(Arkeoloji Müzesi):* 9 a.m. to 5 p.m.; closed Monday.

Atatürk Museum *(Atatürk Müzesi):* 10 to 11.30 a.m., 2 to 4.30 p.m.; closed on the 15th of each month.

Beylerbeyi Palace *(Beylerbeyi Sarayı):* 9.30 a.m. to noon, 1.30 to 4.30 p.m.; closed Monday and Thursday.

Dolmabahçe Palace *(Dolmabahçe Sarayı Müzesi):* 9 a.m. to noon, 1.30 to 4 p.m.; closed Monday and Thursday.

Kilim and Carpet Museum *(Kilim ve Düz Dokuma Yaygılar Müzesi):* 9 a.m. to 5 p.m.; closed Monday.

Maritime Museum *(Deniz Müzesi):* 9 a.m. to noon, 1 to 5.30 p.m.; closed Monday and Tuesday.

Military Museum *(Askeri Müze):* 9 a.m. to noon, 1 to 5 p.m.; closed Monday and Tuesday.

Mosaic Museum *(Mozaik Müzesi):* 9 a.m. to 5 p.m.; closed Monday and Tuesday.

Municipal Museum *(Belediye Müzesi):* 9 a.m. to noon, 1 to 5 p.m.; closed on the 5th of each month.

Oriental Archeology Museum *(Eski Şark Eserleri Müzesi):* 9 a.m. to 5 p.m.; closed Monday and Tuesday.

Painting and Sculpture Museum *(Resim ve Heykel Müzesi):* noon to 4 p.m.; closed Monday and Tuesday.

Rumeli Fortress *(Rumeli Hisarı):* 10 a.m. to 5 p.m.; closed Monday.

St. Saviour in Chora *(Kariye Müzesi):* 9.30 a.m. to 5 p.m.; closed Tuesday.

St. Sophia *(Ayasofya):* 9.30 a.m. to 5 p.m.; closed Monday.

Seven Towers *(Yedikule):* 10 a.m. to 5 p.m.; closed Monday.

Sunken Palace *(Yerebatan Sarayı):* 9 a.m. to 5 p.m.; closed Monday.

Tiled kiosk *(Çinili Köşkü):* 9 a.m. to 5 p.m.; closed Monday.

Topkapı Palace *(Topkapı Sarayı Müzesi):* 9.30 a.m. to 5 p.m.; closed Tuesday.

Turkish and Islamic Arts Museum *(Türk ve İslam Eserleri Müzesi, İbrahim Paşa Sarayı):* 9.30 a.m. to 5 p.m.; closed Monday.

Yıldız Palace *(Yıldız Sarayı):* 9.30 a.m. to 5 p.m.; closed Monday.

Major mosques open before the first prayer at dawn and close after the last prayer at sunset. To visit smaller mosques, including some churches which have been converted into mosques, you may have to ask around for the key.

NEWSPAPERS, MAGAZINES and BOOKS *(gazete, mecmua, kitap).* Bookshops and stationers are usually separate shops. Newsstands in hotels or on the street sell a good selection of foreign papers (available a day or two after publication) and magazines.

The Directorate General of Press and Information publishes a weekly digest, *Newspot,* in Arabic, English, French and German. It is available free of charge from tourist offices.

In Istanbul, one of the main foreign-language bookshops is Haşet Kitapevi, at İstiklâl Caddesi 469 in the main street of the modern city. Stalls at museums and archaeological sites stock excellent publications related to the areas, often translated into foreign languages from Turkish.

Have you any English-language newspapers?	**Bir İngiliz gazeteniz var mı?**

POLICE. (See also EMERGENCIES.) All types of police (city, tourist and traffic) wear similar greenish-grey uniforms with identifying badges. The Tourist Police badge carries the words "Turizm Polisi". In Istanbul, the Tourist Police office is at

Liman Caddesi 100, Kumkapı (tel. 527 45 03).

Where's the nearest police station?	**En yakın karakol nerede?**

PUBLIC HOLIDAYS *(milli bayramlar).* The following are the holidays when banks, schools, offices and shops are closed. The afternoon before a public holiday is often taken off, too.

Jan. 1	*Yılbaşı*	New Year's Day
April 23	*23 Nisan Çocuk Bayramı*	National Independence and Children's Day
May 19	*Gençlik ve Spor Bayramı*	Youth and Sports Day
Aug. 30	*Zafer Bayramı*	Victory Day
Oct. 29	*Cumhuriyet Bayramı*	Republic Day

P Apart from these civic celebrations, there are two important Muslim holy periods which are based on the lunar calendar and occur 10 to 12 days earlier each year. The first follows the four weeks daylight fasting and prayer of Ramadan *(Ramazan)* and is called Şeker Bayramı (Sugar Holy Days), lasting three to five days. Two months and ten days later comes the four-to-five day Kurban Bayramı (Holy Days of Sacrifice) festival. During these periods, normal business is interrupted, and you'll find it very difficult to get places on boats and buses or arrange accommodation.

Are you open tomorrow?   **Yarın açık mısınız?**

R **RADIO and TELEVISION** *(radyo; televizyon).* The Voice of Turkey broadcasts in English on shortwave from 12.30 to 1 p.m. and 8 to 9 p.m. daily. TRT (Turkish Radio and Television) III has news and weather summaries in English, French and German on FM at intervals throughout the day.

Television is not of a high standard, but it does give a look at Turkish life.

RELIGIOUS SERVICES. Turkey is a 99% Muslim country, and churches are only found in major cities. Istanbul, however, has a fair amount of Catholic, Gregorian, Orthodox and Protestant churches, plus half a dozen synagogues. Services in English are held at St. Helena Anglican Church, in the grounds of the British consulate, Meşrutiyet Caddesi 34, and at the Dutch Chapel (Union Church), Postacılar Sokağı 7 (İstiklâl Caddesi).

S **SHOPPING and OFFICE HOURS.** Government and commercial offices are open from 8.30 a.m. to 12.30 p.m. and from 1.30 to 5.30 p.m., Monday to Friday.

Shops normally open 9 a.m. to 7 p.m., Monday to Saturday. Istanbul's Grand Bazaar is open 8.30 a.m. to 7 p.m., closed Sundays, and the Spice Market opens from 8 a.m. to 7 p.m. the same days. On the coast, some establishments are çlosed during the afternoon in the summer, but this doesn't apply to enterprises dealing with tourists.

T **TIME DIFFERENCES.** Turkey follows Eastern European Time, GMT + 2. In summer, clocks are set one hour ahead (GMT + 3).

	New York	London	**Istanbul**	Jo'burg	Sydney	Auckland
winter:	5 a.m.	10 a.m.	**noon**	noon	9 p.m.	11 p.m.
summer:	5 a.m.	10 a.m.	**noon**	11 a.m.	7 p.m.	9 p.m.

What time is it?   **Saat kaç?**

TIPPING. Service charges are generally included in the bill at hotels and restaurants, but a little extra is always appreciated, especially for good service. Quite often, the fee for some services (airport porter, hat check, lavatory, etc.) is signposted. Average tips:

Hotel porter, per bag	500 TL (1,000 TL for 3 bags)
Maid, per week	4,000–5,000 TL
Waiter	5% if service included, 10% if not
Taxi driver	Round up to nearest 300 TL
Tour guide	5% of excursion fare
Hairdresser/Barber	15%

TOILETS *(tuvalet).* Facilities are fine in hotels and large restaurants, acceptable at big highway filling stations, otherwise often below standard. Carry tissues with you when travelling; toilet paper is not always supplied. Men's toilets are indicated by the word "Erkekler" or "Baylar"; women's by "Kadınlar" or "Bayanlar", or recognizable symbols.

Where are the toilets?   **Tuvaletler nerede?**

TOURIST INFORMATION OFFICES *(turizm danışma bürosu).* The Turkish Ministry of Culture and Tourism is represented by the Turkish Tourism and Information Office. Head office:

Gazi Mustafa Kemal Bulvarı 33, Ankara; tel. (4) 229 29 30, ext. 95

Turkish Tourism and Information Offices abroad:

U.K.   170–173 Piccadilly, First Floor, London W1V 9 DD;
                 tel. (01) 734 8681

T **U.S.A.** 821 United Nations Plaza, New York,
NY 10017; tel. (212) 687-2194

In Turkey, every town of any size has a tourist information office.

Istanbul Meşrutiyet Caddesi 57, Kat 6–7, Galatasaray;
tel. (1) 145 65 93
There is also a tourist office at the airport, and at the
Hilton hotels, Karaköy, Yalova and Kocaeli.

Izmir Atatürk Caddesi 418, Alsancak; tel. (51) 21 68 41

Where is the tourist office? **Turizim bürosu nerede?**

TRANSPORT

Buses *(otobüs)* are cheap but often crowded. For city buses, buy a
booklet of tickets at the office behind the main bus stations, then drop
your ticket into the box by the driver. If you don't have a ticket, another passenger will probably help by selling you one. In Istanbul, a
Mavi Kart (Blue Card) available at main terminals allows you to use
the buses for one month from the first day of the month. You need a
photo and your passport for identity and will have to wait a day or two
to pick the card up.

Taxis *(taksi)* are metered in Istanbul and Izmir. They can be identified
by a black-and-yellow chequer band. Have the address written down
to avoid struggling to explain to drivers, who usually speak only Turkish. In Istanbul, the one-way street system may force your driver to
take a circuitous route. Tipping is up to you, but since drivers are generally helpful, add a little.

Dolmuş are shared taxis—a midway solution between taxis and buses.
Black-and-white signs mark official stops, otherwise wait till a car
(usually a big, old American make) slows down, enquire "Dolmuş?"
and name your destination. *Dolmuş* run prescribed routes and will let
you off where you wish along the way. You're crushed in with other
passengers going in the same direction, but it's an inexpensive, effi-
cient system which you can master only through trial and error.

Underground/Subway. Istanbul's useful *Tünel* was designed by a
French engineer in 1875 and updated in 1971, and is still going strong.
124 It runs a short distance of about half a mile from Karaköy towards the
centre of modern Istanbul. Buy your token inside the entrance.

Ferries. Boats leave from Eminönü in old Istanbul for the villages along the Bosphorus and the Golden Horn, and the crossing to Üsküdar on the Asian Coast. For Princes Islands, they set off from Kabatas, early in the morning, then later from Sirkeci. For coastal services and cruises, reserve ahead of time through the Turkish Maritime Lines, which have agents at the quays in all Turkish ports.

Long-distance buses. In Istanbul, coaches and minibuses leave from Topkapı Otogarı (not to be confused with Topkapı Palace in quite another area of the city), the Central Bus Station. The station is divided into two sections, the Trakya Otogarı for buses going west and the Anadolu Otogarı for eastbound buses (which also have a terminal at Harem on the Asian side). Inter-city buses are generally faster than the railway and relatively inexpensive. Choose a modern, air-conditioned vehicle.

Trains. The Turkish State Railways (TCDD) run fast, comfortable trains on some major routes. Long-distance trains have sleeping and dining cars. Among the best are the *Mavi Tren (Blue Train),* daily between Istanbul and Ankara (7½ hours), and the *Boğaziçi Ekspresi,* also daily between Istanbul and Ankara (9½ hours). Istanbul has two railway stations: Sirkeci Garı (Europe) for westbound trains and Haydarpaşa Garı (Asia) for eastbound trains.

Where's the nearest bus/dolmuş stop?	**En yakın otobüs/dolmuş durağı nerededir?**
When's the next ferryboat/ bus/train to ...?	**... bir sonra ki vapur/otobüs/ tren saat kaçta?**
I want a ticket to ...	**...'(a) bir bilet istiyorum.**
single (one-way)	**gidiş**
return (round-trip)	**gidiş-dönüş**
first/second class	**birinci/ikinci mevki**
What's the fare to ...?	**... için ücret nedir?**
Will you tell me when to get off?	**Ne zaman inmem gerektiğini söyler misiniz?**

WATER *(su).* Tap water is heavily chlorinated, therefore safe to drink but unpleasant in taste. Bottled water, either fizzy (carbonated) or still, is a more agreeable, inexpensive alternative.

I'd like a bottle of mineral water.	**Bir şişe maden suyu istiyorum.**
fizzy/still	**soda/su**

SOME USEFUL EXPRESSIONS

yes/no	evet/hayır
please/thank you	lütfen/teşekkür ederim
excuse me	affedersiniz
where/when/how	nerede/ne zaman/nasıl
how long/how far	ne kadar sürer/ne kadar mesafede
yesterday/today/tomorrow	dün/bugün/yarın
day/week/month/year	gün/hafta/ay/yıl
left/right	sol/sağ
right/wrong	doğru/yanlış
big/small	büyük/küçük
cheap/expensive	ucuz/pahalı
old/new	eski/yeni
good/bad	iyi/kötü
hot/cold	sıcak/soğuk
open/closed	açık/kapalı
free (vacant)/occupied	boş/meşgul
no vacancy/no rooms	boş yer yok/boş oda yok
entrance/exit	giriş/çıkış
push/pull	itiniz/çekiniz
Waiter/Waitress, please.	Garson/Hanımefendi, lütfen.
I'd like...	...istiyorum.
How much is that?	Bu kaça?

NUMBERS

0	sıfır	13	onüç	50	elli
1	bir	14	ondört	60	altmış
2	iki	15	onbeş	70	yetmiş
3	üç	16	onaltı	80	seksen
4	dört	17	onyedi	90	doksan
5	beş	18	onsekiz	100	yüz
6	altı	19	ondokuz	101	yüzbir
7	yedi	20	yirmi	126	yüzyirmialtı
8	sekiz	21	yirmibir	200	ikiyüz
9	dokuz	22	yirmiiki	300	üçyüz
10	on	23	yirmiüç	1,000	bin
11	onbir	30	otuz	2,500	ikibinbeşyüz
12	oniki	40	kırk		

Index

An asterisk (*) next to a page number indicates a map reference. Where there is more than one set of page references, the one in bold type refers to the main entry. For index to Practical Information, see inside front cover.